PERFORMANCE WHISPERER

UNLOCKING
THE *FULL POTENTIAL*
OF THOSE YOU LEAD

PERFORMANCE WHISPERER

Chad T. Dyar

PALMETTO
PUBLISHING
Charleston, SC
www.PalmettoPublishing.com

Paperback ISBN: 979-8-8229-5925-5

Dedication

To my mentors and coaches, who have guided me with wisdom, empathy, and unwavering support.

To all the individuals I've had the privilege to coach. Your dedication, resilience, and commitment to growth have been my greatest inspiration.

To my family, for their constant love and support. Your belief in me has been the foundation of my success.

To my colleagues and the entire professional community, who continually strive for excellence and innovation.

This book is for all of you who believe in the transformative power of coaching and continuous improvement. Thank you for inspiring me to unlock the potential in myself and others.

Table of Contents

A Personal Note from the Author

Thank you for picking up *Performance Whisperer*. This book is a culmination of my journey, experiences, and passion for coaching and personal development. My aim is to share with you the insights and tools that have shaped my approach to coaching and, hopefully, inspire you to unlock the potential in yourself and others.

I've always been fascinated by the power of coaching. Before I ever had a manager, I had a little league coach and a vocal coach, and I'm not sure which of my coaches was tougher. Coaching has always represented a unique blend of art and science for me, requiring empathy, skill, and a deep understanding of human potential that can be used to motivate and drive optimal performance . Throughout my career, I've witnessed firsthand how effective coaching can transform lives, enhance performance (whether it was baseball, vocal performance or on the job performance), and create a culture and mindset of continuous growth.

In *Performance Whisperer*, I explore the core elements of coaching pivotal to my journey. You will see familiar concepts and some alchemy as I've worked to apply all the methods and techniques I've learned into coaching. We delve into the importance of inspiration—how a single word or gesture can ignite a spark and propel someone towards greatness. We examine the practical aspects of coaching, providing actionable strategies and exercises you can implement immediately. From practicing basic empathy to goal-setting frameworks, this book is designed to be your comprehensive guide to effective coaching.

One of the most significant lessons I've learned is the impact of professional courage and honesty. Coaching is not just about guiding others through easy times but also standing by them during challenging moments. It's about having tough conversations, making difficult decisions, and always striving for improvement. In this book, I share stories and examples of how embracing professional courage can lead to remarkable outcomes.

Empathy, balance, and professional courage are recurring themes in this book. They are the pillars of my coaching philosophy and have been instrumental in my personal and professional growth. By focusing on these areas, I believe we can create an environment where individuals feel empowered to explore, learn, and excel.

As you embark on this journey with me, I encourage you to bring your best self to the process. Coaching is a dynamic and reciprocal relationship; the more you invest in it, the more you will gain. Whether you are a seasoned coach or just starting, I hope this book provides you with valuable insights and practical tools to enhance your coaching practice.

Thank you for allowing me to share my vision and experiences with you. I am excited to see how you will apply these principles and make a difference in your own life and the lives of those you coach.

Introduction

Welcome to *Performance Whisperer*.

I am thrilled to take you on this journey through the transformative world of coaching. This book is a culmination of my experiences, insights, and passion for helping individuals unlock their true potential. From my early days as a stage performer to my current role as an Enablement leader, I've always been fascinated by the power of coaching to inspire, motivate, and drive performance.

Coaching, in its essence, is about more than just providing guidance; it's about creating an environment where individuals can thrive. It's about understanding the unique needs of each person and tailoring your approach to meet those needs. This book is structured around three core pillars: coaching like a human (focusing on empathy), coaching skill (focusing on professional development), and coaching performance (goal setting and continuous improvement). These pillars form the foundation of effective coaching and will guide our exploration throughout this book.

In *Performance Whisperer*, I will share stories, techniques, and practical exercises that have shaped my coaching philosophy. We will delve into the importance of empathy, balance, and professional courage. You'll learn how to inspire others, develop actionable coaching strategies, and create a culture of continuous growth and improvement. I will include detailed scenarios and examples throughout. My goal is to provide you with the tools and insights needed to become an effective coach and to help those you coach achieve their highest potential. I will be throwing a lot at you in the coming pages. As I was putting this book together, I realized how full my coaching arsenal has become over the last 30+ years. Use what is most helpful to you for wherever you are on your coaching journey. I have used and trained on all of these techniques at some point or another in my career. I have never used them ALL in one place (nor am I certain that I actually could). I will keep my examples focused on the workplace. While I am sure some of my experiences as a vocal coach or being vocally coached may be evocative, I want to keep the content of this book as universally relevant as possible. This book will be full of examples of each of the frameworks and techniques I share and although the examples are based on real people and situations, I have changed names and some of the descriptive elements to be respectful of the people the examples are based on.

Throughout this book, I also draw on principles learned from my experiences with Lean Six Sigma, Design Thinking, Change Management, and Executive Communication to further enrich your coaching practice. These methodologies are not just theoretical frameworks but practical tools that have been instrumental in my own journey and part of realizing my goal of continuous learning. They will help you approach coaching with creativity, manage transitions effectively, and communicate with clarity and impact. I have also thrown in some bonus content on a few additional skills that I believe prepare you to be a better coach and leader including techniques for problem solving and communication principles. If this feels like the kitchen sink of Coaching information, that's because in my world, it is!

As a seasoned enablement leader, I've seen firsthand the profound impact that thoughtful, empathetic coaching can have on individuals and organizations. My enablement philosophy is rooted in three core principles: know your customers (empathy), know your products (knowledge/skill), and know your process (performance). By deeply understanding these elements, you can tailor your coaching approach to meet the unique needs of each coachee and drive meaningful results for your business.

As you read through these pages, I encourage you to reflect on your own coaching journey. Think about the moments that have shaped you, the challenges you've faced, and the successes you've achieved. Use this book as a guide to enhance your coaching practice and to inspire others to bring their best selves to every endeavor.

Thank you for joining me on this journey. Let's unlock the power of coaching together and transform the way we lead, inspire, and drive performance across the diverse people and teams we coach.

My "Why"

A Transformative Coaching Experience

Early in my career, as an opera singer transitioning into the business world, I found myself navigating unfamiliar territory. It was a period of immense change and uncertainty, but also one of profound growth and discovery. One pivotal moment came when I was coached by Priscilla Winley, my manager at Toshiba Corporation. Priscilla was both a powerful coach and a challenging manager, holding me to a higher standard than I had ever experienced. She not only unlocked my potential but also gave me the freedom to create a path that worked for me.

I vividly remember the day I walked into Priscilla's office, feeling overwhelmed by the challenges ahead. She greeted me with a warm smile and an open heart, instantly putting me at ease. Her office was a reflection of her coaching style—organized yet inviting, with personal touches that made it feel like a safe space for honest conversations. A poster behind her desk read, "Inspect what you expect." This motto emphasized that coaching, advice, and commands are never enough without consistency, follow-up, and celebration of every milestone.

Our first coaching sessions focused on understanding my strengths and areas for improvement. Priscilla used techniques like SWOT analysis and 360-degree feedback to paint a comprehensive picture of my professional self. This was my first introduction to these tools, and their impact was immediate. For the first time, I saw a clear path forward, illuminated by my strengths and the support of a dedicated coach.

One session stands out in my memory. We discussed my tendency to take on too much at once, often leading to burnout. Instead of simply telling me to manage my time better, Priscilla guided me through an exercise. She encouraged me to empathize with my own needs, define clear goals, ideate solutions, prototype new habits, and test them. This approach was a game-changer. It wasn't just about managing time; it was about redesigning my approach to work and life.

Priscilla also taught me the power of effective communication. During one session, we practiced crafting clear, concise messages that could resonate with different audiences. This skill became invaluable as I moved into leadership roles, where the ability to communicate effectively is often the difference between success and failure. Having great ideas is not enough to get buy-in. Great communication skills are required to inform, involve, and incite people to action.

But perhaps the most significant lesson I learned from Priscilla was the importance of empathy and trust. She modeled these qualities in every interaction, showing me that true leadership and coaching are built on understanding and mutual respect. Her empathetic approach made it easy for me to open up about my fears and aspirations, creating a partnership that was both supportive and challenging.

This coaching experience transformed my career and inspired my passion for coaching others. It taught me that coaching is not about providing answers but about guiding others to find their own. It's about asking the right questions, listening deeply, and fostering a sense of trust and collaboration. These principles have become the cornerstone of my coaching philosophy and are woven throughout the fabric of this book.

Every day, I strive to bring the same level of empathy, skill, and courage to my coaching relationships that Priscilla brought to ours. Her belief in my potential ignited a spark in me that continues to burn brightly. It is my hope that through this book, I can pass on that spark to you, helping you unlock the full potential of those you lead.

Part 1

Coaching Like a Human (Focusing on Empathy)

CHAPTER 1

The Heart of Coaching—Empathy

"Empathy is about finding echoes of another person in yourself."
—Mohsin Hamid

Empathy is the cornerstone of effective coaching. It allows you to connect with your coachee on a deeper level, fostering trust and understanding. In this chapter, you will learn why empathy is crucial in coaching, how to develop your empathic abilities, and the impact it can have on your coaching relationships.

Why Empathy is Crucial in Coaching

Empathy is the ability to understand and share the feelings of another person. In the context of coaching, it means being able to put yourself in your coachee's shoes, seeing the world from their perspective, and acknowledging their emotions and experiences. In order to do this you have to be willing to lay down your agenda, use your powers of deep discovery, and pay attention to what you see, hear and feel as you get to know the people you will be coaching.

Building Trust and Rapport

Trust is the foundation of any successful coaching relationship. When coachees feel understood and valued, they are more likely to open up and engage in the coaching process. Empathy helps build this trust by showing that you genuinely care about their well-being and success. We will explore several ways to build trust and rapport in chapter 2.

Enhancing Communication

Effective communication is a two-way street. By being empathetic, you not only listen to what your coachee is saying but also understand the emotions behind their words. This deeper level of understanding allows for more meaningful and productive conversations.

Encouraging Self-Reflection and Growth

Empathy fosters a safe environment where coachees feel comfortable exploring their thoughts and feelings. This encourages self-reflection, which is essential for personal growth. When coachees know that they are supported and not judged, they are more likely to take risks, experiment with new behaviors, and learn from their experiences.

Self-reflection is a powerful tool that can lead to profound personal and professional growth. It involves taking the time to thoughtfully consider your actions, thoughts, and experiences to gain deeper insights and understandings. In this chapter, we will explore the importance of self-reflection, techniques to develop this skill, and how it contributes to continuous growth.

The Importance of Self-Reflection

Self-reflection allows you to pause and think deeply about your experiences and behaviors. This process is crucial for personal and professional development because it helps you identify areas of strength and areas that need improvement. Without reflection, it's easy to fall into patterns of behavior that may be unproductive or even harmful.

Here are some key benefits of self-reflection:

1. **Enhanced Self-Awareness**: By regularly reflecting on your actions and decisions, you become more aware of your strengths, weaknesses, and the impact you have on others.
2. **Improved Decision-Making**: Self-reflection helps you learn from past experiences, leading to better decision-making in the future.
3. **Greater Emotional Intelligence**: Reflecting on your emotions and reactions increases your emotional intelligence, helping you manage your emotions and respond effectively to others.
4. **Continuous Learning**: Self-reflection fosters a mindset of continuous learning and improvement, which is essential for growth and development.

Techniques for Effective Self-Reflection

Self-reflection is a skill that can be developed and refined over time. Here are some techniques to help you get started:

1. **Journaling**: Writing down your thoughts and experiences is a powerful way to reflect. Keep a journal where you record your daily activities, feelings, and reflections. Reviewing your entries can provide valuable insights and patterns.
2. **Mindfulness Meditation**: Practicing mindfulness meditation helps you become more aware of your thoughts and feelings in the present moment. This awareness can lead to deeper self-reflection and understanding.
3. **Feedback from Others**: Seeking feedback from trusted colleagues, friends, or mentors can provide an outside perspective

on your behavior and actions. Use this feedback to reflect on areas where you can improve.

4. **Regular Reflection Time:** Set aside dedicated time each day or week for reflection. Use this time to think about your recent experiences, what you learned, and how you can apply those lessons moving forward.

5. **Questioning:** Ask yourself reflective questions to gain deeper insights. Questions like "What went well today?", "What could I have done differently?" and "What did I learn from this experience?" can prompt meaningful reflection.

Applying Self-Reflection for Growth

Once you have developed the habit of self-reflection, the next step is to use the insights gained to foster growth and development. Here's how to apply self-reflection for continuous growth:

1. **Set Personal Goals:** Use your reflections to set personal and professional goals. Identify areas where you want to improve and create specific, actionable goals to achieve them.

2. **Develop Action Plans:** For each goal, develop a detailed action plan outlining the steps you need to take. Regularly review and adjust your plans based on your reflections and progress.

3. **Embrace Change:** Be open to change and willing to adapt. Self-reflection often highlights areas where change is needed. Embrace these opportunities to grow and improve.

4. **Celebrate Successes:** Acknowledge and celebrate your achievements, no matter how small. Recognizing your progress boosts motivation and reinforces the benefits of self-reflection.

5. **Learn from Mistakes:** View mistakes and setbacks as learning opportunities. Reflect on what went wrong, why it happened, and how you can prevent similar issues in the future.

Developing Your Empathic Abilities

Empathy is a skill that can be cultivated and strengthened over time. Here are some strategies to help you develop your empathic abilities:

Active Listening

Active listening involves fully concentrating, understanding, and responding thoughtfully to what your coachee is saying. Techniques to enhance active listening include maintaining eye contact, nodding, and summarizing what the coachee has said to ensure understanding. Chapter 3 will focus on helping you build this muscle.

Practicing Emotional Intelligence

Emotional intelligence is the ability to recognize, understand, and manage your own emotions, as well as the emotions of others. Developing emotional intelligence involves being aware of your emotional triggers and practicing self-regulation. It also includes being able to read and respond to the emotions of your coachee.

Empathy Mapping

Empathy mapping is a tool that helps you visualize your coachee's thoughts, feelings, and experiences. By creating an empathy map, you can gain a clearer understanding of their perspective and identify areas where they may need support.

Step-by-Step Guide to Building an Empathy Map

Step 1: Gather Materials
- Large paper or whiteboard
- Markers or sticky notes
- Empathy map template (optional)

Step 2: Understand the Sections of an Empathy Map

An empathy map is typically divided into four main quadrants, each focusing on different aspects of the coachee's experience. These quadrants are:

1. **Says**
2. **Thinks**
3. **Does**
4. **Feels**

Step 3: Define the Persona

Identify who the empathy map is for. This could be a specific coachee or a composite persona representing a group of coachees with similar characteristics.

Step 4: Fill in the Quadrants

1. **Says**
   - Write down what the coachee explicitly says in conversations, meetings, or coaching sessions.
   - Example: "I'm struggling to keep up with my workload."

2. **Thinks**
   - Capture what the coachee might be thinking but not necessarily saying out loud.
   - Example: "I'm worried I won't meet my targets."

3. **Does**
   - Note the coachee's observable actions and behaviors.
   - Example: Works late hours, frequently checks emails.

4. **Feels**
   - Identify the coachee's emotional state based on their words, body language, and behaviors.
   - Example: Overwhelmed, anxious, frustrated.

Step 5: Add Details and Insights
- Use specific examples and observations to add depth to each quadrant.
- Involve the coachee in the process if possible to gain accurate insights.

Step 6: Identify Pain Points and Opportunities
- Look for recurring themes or significant insights that indicate the coachee's main challenges and areas for growth.
- Example: Pain Point: Struggles with time management. Opportunity: Time management training.

Step 7: Review and Validate
- Review the empathy map with the coachee or team to ensure accuracy and completeness.
- Make adjustments based on feedback and additional insights.

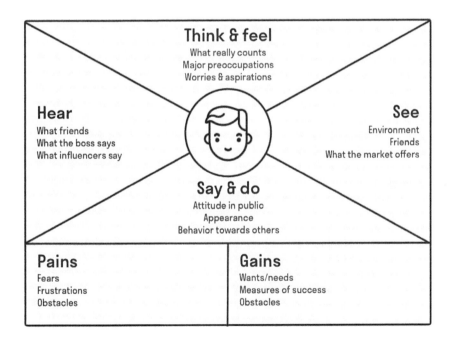

Example Empathy Map

Persona: Jane, a Sales Manager

Says	Thinks	Does	Feels
"I'm struggling to keep up with my workload."	"I'm worried I won't meet my targets."	Works late hours	Overwhelmed
"I need more support from my team."	"Why can't I manage my time better?"	Frequently checks emails	Anxious
"There's too much on my plate."	"Am I good enough for this role?"	Cancels personal plans	Frustrated

Benefits of Using an Empathy Map

- **Enhanced Understanding:** Gain deeper insights into the coachee's perspective.
- **Improved Communication:** Foster open and empathetic communication.
- **Tailored Coaching:** Develop more effective and personalized coaching strategies.
- **Problem-Solving:** Identify root causes of challenges and opportunities for improvement.

Creating an empathy map is a valuable exercise in developing a deeper understanding of your coachee. By visualizing their thoughts, feelings, actions, and words, you can tailor your coaching approach to better support their growth and development. Use the insights gained from the empathy map to foster stronger relationships, address challenges, and create a more supportive coaching environment.

Bonus Content

How to Create a User Manual and Its Benefits in Coaching Relationships

Creating a user manual is an invaluable tool for fostering strong, effective coaching relationships. A user manual provides a comprehensive guide to your personal and professional preferences, working styles, and expectations. This document can serve as a roadmap for your coachees, helping them understand how to interact with you effectively, what drives your decisions, and how to best collaborate with you. It is also a great activity for them as they build their own guide to share with their leader and their team.

Steps to Create a User Manual:

1. **Core Values:**
   - List your fundamental beliefs and guiding principles.
   - Example: "Commitment to continuous improvement," "Creating a safe space for growth."

2. **Operating Principles:**
   - Outline the principles that govern your professional conduct.
   - Example: "Communication is key," "Collaboration is critical."

3. **Expectations:**
   - Specify what you expect from your coachees and team members.
   - Example: "Schedule regular one-on-one meetings," "Bring challenge cards to meetings."

4. **Working Styles:**
   - ◦ Describe your preferred working styles and how you manage tasks.
   - ◦ Example: "Kinesthetic learner by preference," "Visual, auditory, reading and writing methods for teaching."

5. **Strengths and Assessments:**
   - ◦ Include insights from personality and strengths assessments (e.g., StrengthsFinder, Myers-Briggs).
   - ◦ Example: "Top 5 StrengthsFinder themes," "Enneagram type."

6. **Personal Preferences:**
   - ◦ Share personal details that can help in building rapport.
   - ◦ Example: Hobbies, favorite foods, beverages, and fun facts.

Benefits of a User Manual in Coaching:

Creating and sharing a user manual at the beginning of a new coaching relationship lays the groundwork for a successful partnership by providing enhanced understanding, improved communication, building trust, and effective collaboration. It offers a clear understanding of your values, expectations, and working styles, helping coachees know how to interact with you effectively. It sets the tone for open and honest communication, facilitating transparent discussions about preferences and expectations. Additionally, it demonstrates your commitment to the relationship, establishing a foundation of mutual respect and understanding. Streamlining collaboration by aligning goals and working styles ensures everyone is on the same page regarding processes and expectations. This tool helps in setting clear expectations, fostering open communication, and building a strong, trusting relationship with your coachees.

Building Relationships

Building strong relationships with your coachees requires time and effort, as it is foundational to effective coaching. Engage in activities that foster trust and rapport, such as sharing personal stories, being transparent about your intentions, and consistently following through on your commitments. Strong relationships foster trust, open communication, and mutual respect, which are essential for a productive coaching partnership.

1. **Initial Meeting: Set the Stage**
   - **Introduce Yourself:** Share your background, coaching philosophy, and what they can expect from the coaching relationship.
   - **Learn About Them:** Ask about their background, goals, and any previous coaching experiences.

2. **Establish Trust and Rapport**
   - **Be Authentic:** Show genuine interest in their well-being and development.
   - **Confidentiality:** Assure them that your conversations are private and confidential.

3. **Active Listening**
   - **Fully Engage:** Listen without interrupting, maintain eye contact, and show that you value their input.
   - **Reflect and Clarify:** Paraphrase what they've said to ensure understanding and show that you're paying attention.

4. **Empathy and Understanding**
   - **Understand Their Perspective:** Try to see things from their point of view.
   - **Be Compassionate:** Show empathy towards their challenges and successes.

5. **Set Clear Expectations**
   - **Define Roles:** Clarify what they can expect from you and what you expect from them.
   - **Agree on Goals:** Establish clear, achievable goals together.

6. **Create a Safe Environment**
   - **Be Non-Judgmental:** Ensure they feel safe sharing their thoughts and feelings without fear of judgment.
   - **Encourage Openness:** Promote honest and open communication.

7. **Be Consistent and Reliable**
   - **Follow Through:** Always keep your promises and commitments.
   - **Regular Check-ins:** Schedule consistent meetings and be punctual.

8. **Provide Constructive Feedback**
   - **Be Specific and Actionable:** Use frameworks like the SBI model to provide clear and actionable feedback.
   - **Balance Positive and Negative:** Highlight strengths and successes as well as areas for improvement.

9. **Personal Connection**
   - **Share Personal Stories:** Occasionally sharing relevant personal experiences can help build rapport.
   - **Celebrate Milestones:** Acknowledge and celebrate their achievements and progress.

10. **Be Patient and Persistent**
   - **Building Trust Takes Time:** Understand that building a strong relationship doesn't happen overnight.
   - **Stay Committed:** Show continuous dedication to their growth and development.

Seeking Feedback

Regularly seek feedback from your coachees about your coaching style and the level of empathy you demonstrate. Use this feedback to make adjustments and continuously improve your empathic abilities.

To continuously improve your coaching and empathy skills, it's essential to establish a regular feedback loop with your coachees. Here's how you can do it effectively:

1. **Schedule Regular Feedback Sessions:** Set up periodic check-ins specifically for gathering feedback. These can be monthly or quarterly, depending on your coaching frequency and the needs of your coachees.

2. **Create a Safe Environment:** Ensure that your coachees feel comfortable and safe sharing their honest opinions. Emphasize that their feedback is valuable and will be used to enhance their coaching experience.

3. **Ask Specific Questions:** Develop a set of specific questions that target your coaching style and empathy. For example:
   ◦ "Can you describe a recent coaching session and how you felt about my approach?"
   ◦ "In what ways do you feel I show empathy during our sessions?"
   ◦ "Are there any areas where you think I could improve in understanding and responding to your needs?"

4. **Use Anonymous Surveys:** Sometimes, coachees may feel more comfortable providing honest feedback anonymously. Consider using online survey tools to gather detailed insights.

5. **Listen Actively:** During feedback sessions, practice active listening. Show that you value their input by summarizing what they've said and asking follow-up questions to gain deeper understanding.

6. **Reflect on Feedback:** After gathering feedback, take time to reflect on it. Identify common themes and areas for improvement. Consider both the positive feedback and the constructive criticism.

7. **Develop an Action Plan:** Based on the feedback, create a specific action plan to address the areas for improvement. Set clear, measurable goals for yourself and outline the steps you will take to achieve them.

8. **Communicate Changes:** Let your coachees know the changes you plan to implement based on their feedback. This demonstrates that you value their input and are committed to continuous improvement.

9. **Monitor Progress:** Regularly assess your progress in the areas you've identified for improvement. Seek ongoing feedback to ensure that the changes you've made are having the desired effect.

10. **Iterate and Adapt:** Coaching and empathy are dynamic skills that evolve over time. Continuously seek feedback, reflect, and adapt your approach to stay aligned with the needs of your coachees.

By systematically seeking and acting on feedback, you can enhance your empathic abilities and become a more effective coach, ultimately fostering stronger, more productive coaching relationships.

The Impact of Empathy on Coaching Relationships

Empathy has a profound impact on the effectiveness of coaching relationships. Here are some key benefits:

Strengthened Trust

When coachees feel understood and valued, they are more likely to trust you and the coaching process. This trust creates a strong foundation for open and honest communication.

Increased Engagement

Empathy helps to create a supportive and non-judgmental environment. Coachees are more likely to engage fully in the coaching process when they feel safe and understood.

Enhanced Problem-Solving

By understanding your coachee's perspective, you can better guide them in exploring solutions to their challenges. Empathy allows you to ask insightful questions that encourage deeper thinking and innovative problem-solving.

Improved Outcomes

Coaching relationships built on empathy are more likely to result in positive outcomes. When coachees feel supported and understood, they are more motivated to take action and achieve their goals.

Long-Lasting Relationships

Empathy fosters long-lasting relationships that extend beyond the coaching sessions. Coachees are more likely to view you as a trusted advisor and continue to seek your guidance in the future.

Scenario: Jane's Empathic Approach

Meet Jane, a sales manager who is struggling with low team morale. Despite her best efforts, her usual motivational tactics, like offering bonuses and public recognition, seem to be falling flat. Team meetings are marked by disengagement, and performance metrics are steadily declining. Jane realizes that something deeper is affecting her team's spirit.

Determined to get to the root of the problem, Jane decides to practice empathy. She schedules one-on-one meetings with each team member, dedicating time to genuinely listen to their concerns and experiences.

Meeting with Penny: During her meeting with Penny, Jane learns that Penny has been feeling overwhelmed by the recent increase in workload due to a colleague's sudden departure. Penny is juggling multiple responsibilities and feels unsupported.

Meeting with Max: Max, another team member, shares that he is dealing with a family health crisis, which has been affecting his focus and productivity at work. He appreciates the job but is struggling to balance personal and professional demands.

Meeting with Dave: Dave reveals that he feels undervalued. Despite his hard work, he believes his contributions go unnoticed, and he's unsure about his career progression within the company.

Jane takes detailed notes during these meetings and thanks each team member for their honesty. She empathizes with their situations and assures them that their concerns are valid and will be addressed.

Action Plan:
1. **For Penny:** Jane arranges additional support by redistributing some of the workload among other team members and hires a temporary assistant to help cover the gap left by the departed colleague.

2. **For Max:** Jane offers flexible working hours and the option to work from home a few days a week, giving Max the ability to manage his family responsibilities more effectively.
3. **For Dave:** Jane sets up a recognition program that highlights individual contributions during team meetings and begins discussing career development plans with Dave a to outline a clear path for his growth.

Outcome: Within a few weeks, Jane observes a remarkable change in her team's morale. Penny feels less overwhelmed and more supported, leading to increased productivity. Max appreciates the flexibility, which allows him to handle his personal matters without sacrificing his professional responsibilities. Dave feels more recognized and motivated, with a clear sense of his future in the company.

By practicing empathy, Jane was able to understand the unique challenges each team member faced and tailor her coaching methods accordingly. This approach not only boosted team morale but also improved overall performance, demonstrating the profound impact of empathetic leadership.

Call to Action

- Identify a recent coaching session and reflect on how empathy was (or wasn't) demonstrated.
- Write down two ways you can incorporate more empathy into your next coaching conversation.

Your Notes:

_____

_____

_____

_____

_____

Models and Techniques

Active Listening
- **Origin:** Popularized by Carl Rogers and Richard Farson in their work on client-centered therapy in the 1950s.
- **Usage:** Enhances communication and understanding between coach and coachee.
- **Description:** Active Listening involves fully concentrating on, understanding, responding to, and remembering what the coachee says. Techniques include maintaining eye contact, nodding, paraphrasing, summarizing, and asking open-ended questions.

Emotional Intelligence
- **Origin:** Developed by psychologists such as Daniel Goleman in the 1990s.
- **Usage:** Enhances your ability to manage emotions and respond empathetically.
- **Description:** Emotional intelligence involves being aware of your own emotions and recognizing those of others. It includes self-regulation, motivation, empathy, and social skills.

Empathy Mapping
- **Origin:** Developed by Dave Gray and his team at XPLANE.
- **Usage:** Used to visualize and understand the feelings, thoughts, and experiences of coachees.
- **Description:** Empathy Mapping involves creating a visual representation of the coachee's internal state. It typically includes quadrants for what the coachee says, thinks, feels, and does.

Trust-Building Activities

- **Origin:** Various, common in team-building and leadership training.
- **Usage:** To create a foundation of trust and strong relationships between coach and coachee.
- **Description:** Activities that promote transparency, reliability, and personal connection. Examples include sharing personal stories, being open about intentions, and consistently following through on commitments.

By integrating empathy into your coaching practice, you can build stronger, more effective relationships with your coachees. Empathy allows you to connect on a deeper level, foster trust, and create an environment where individuals feel valued and motivated to achieve their goals. As you continue on your coaching journey, remember that empathy is not just a skill but a fundamental aspect of being human. Embrace it, develop it, and watch the transformative power it brings to your coaching relationships.

Use this chapter as a guide to enhance your empathic abilities and strengthen your coaching practice. Reflect on your experiences, practice the techniques, and strive to bring empathy into every coaching conversation. By doing so, you will not only become a more effective coach but also make a meaningful impact on the lives of those you lead.

CHAPTER 2

Building Trust and Rapport

"Trust is the glue of life. It's the most essential ingredient in effective communication. It's the foundational principle that holds all relationships."

—Stephen R. Covey

B uilding trust and rapport is the next step in creating a successful coaching relationship. Trust is essential for open communication and effective coaching. In this chapter, you will learn techniques to build trust, the importance of establishing rapport, and how these elements contribute to a productive coaching environment.

The Importance of Trust and Rapport in Coaching

Trust and rapport are the bedrock of any effective coaching relationship. Without them, coachees may be hesitant to share their true thoughts and feelings, limiting the coach's ability to provide meaningful guidance and support. Trust and rapport create a safe space where coachees feel valued, understood, and open to receiving feedback and exploring new ideas.

Trust as the Foundation

Trust is the belief that someone is reliable, truthful, and has your best interests at heart. In coaching, trust means that the coachee believes in the coach's competence, integrity, and genuine desire to help. Trust is built over time through consistent actions and behaviors that demonstrate reliability and care.

Rapport as the Connection

Rapport is a harmonious relationship characterized by mutual understanding and respect. It involves creating a positive and supportive connection where both parties feel comfortable and engaged. Establishing rapport helps to break down barriers, making it easier for the coachee to open up and engage fully in the coaching process.

Techniques to Build Trust and Rapport

Building trust and rapport requires intentional actions and behaviors. Here are some techniques to help you establish and strengthen these crucial elements in your coaching relationships:

Be Genuine and Authentic

Authenticity is key to building trust. Coachees can sense when someone is being genuine, and this authenticity fosters trust. Share your own experiences and be open about your intentions. Show your true self, including your vulnerabilities, to create a deeper connection.

Active Listening

Active listening involves fully focusing on the coachee, understanding their message, and responding thoughtfully. This shows that you value their input and are genuinely interested in their perspective. Techniques to enhance active listening include maintaining eye contact, nodding, paraphrasing, and summarizing what the coachee has said.

Show Empathy

Empathy is the ability to understand and share the feelings of another person. Demonstrating empathy shows that you care about the coachee's experiences and emotions. Practice empathy by acknowledging their feelings, validating their experiences, and offering support.

Be Consistent and Reliable

Consistency and reliability are crucial for building trust. Follow through on your commitments and be punctual for coaching sessions. When coachees see that you are dependable, their trust in you will grow.

Share Personal Stories

Sharing relevant personal stories can help build rapport by showing that you understand and relate to the coachee's experiences. Personal stories make you more relatable and human, fostering a deeper connection.

Establish Clear Boundaries

Setting clear boundaries helps to create a safe and professional coaching environment. Discuss and agree on the boundaries of your coaching relationship, including confidentiality, time commitments, and expectations. Clear boundaries build trust by ensuring that both parties understand and respect each other's limits.

Provide Constructive Feedback

Constructive feedback helps coachees grow and develop. Use the SBI (Situation-Behavior-Impact) model to provide clear, specific, and actionable feedback. This model involves describing the specific situation, detailing the observable behavior, and explaining the impact of that behavior. Constructive feedback builds trust by showing that you are invested in the coachee's improvement.

The Role of Trust and Rapport in a Productive Coaching Environment

Trust and rapport contribute significantly to a productive coaching environment. When coachees trust their coach and feel a strong rapport, they are more likely to engage fully in the coaching process. This engagement leads to more open communication, deeper self-reflection, and greater willingness to take risks and try new behaviors.

Enhanced Communication

Trust and rapport create a safe space for open and honest communication. Coachees feel comfortable sharing their true thoughts and feelings, which allows the coach to provide more targeted and effective guidance.

Increased Motivation and Commitment

When coachees feel understood and supported, they are more motivated to engage in the coaching process and commit to their development goals. Trust and rapport enhance their sense of accountability and drive to succeed.

Greater Resilience

A strong coaching relationship built on trust and rapport helps coachees navigate challenges and setbacks. They feel supported and encouraged to persevere, knowing that their coach is there to help them overcome obstacles.

Improved Outcomes

Coaching relationships characterized by trust and rapport are more likely to result in positive outcomes. Coachees are more willing to take action, implement feedback, and make meaningful changes when they feel supported and understood.

Scenario: John's Trust-Building Journey

John, a new team leader, has been given the challenging task of turning around a struggling department. On his first day, he notices that the team is wary, uncommunicative, and hesitant to engage in meetings. The atmosphere is tense, and productivity is low. John realizes that before he can implement any changes, he needs to build trust and rapport with his team.

Initial Approach: To break the ice, John calls for a team meeting but instead of diving straight into work-related topics, he starts by introducing himself on a personal level. He shares his career journey, including his struggles and successes. John talks about a time when he faced similar challenges in his previous role and how he overcame them.

Sharing Personal Experiences: John openly discusses the mistakes he made and the lessons he learned, emphasizing that he is not there to judge but to support and work alongside his team. He mentions his goals for the department and expresses his confidence in the team's potential to achieve them.

Transparent Intentions: John makes it clear that his intentions are to understand the team's perspective, identify the root causes of the department's struggles, and collaboratively find solutions. He assures them that their opinions and experiences are valuable and necessary for the turnaround process.

One-on-One Meetings: To further build rapport, John schedules one-on-one meetings with each team member. During these sessions, he asks about their personal and professional backgrounds, their views on the current challenges, and their ideas for improvements. John listens actively, taking notes and showing genuine interest in their feedback.

Implementing Feedback: Based on the insights gathered from these meetings, John begins to make small changes that reflect the team's input. He also sets up regular team-building activities to foster a sense of camaraderie and openness.

Outcome: Gradually, John notices a shift in the team's behavior. Team members start to open up, sharing their thoughts and concerns more freely during meetings. They become more engaged in discussions, offering suggestions and collaborating on solutions. The atmosphere in the department becomes more positive, and the team's productivity begins to improve.

By sharing his own experiences and being transparent about his intentions, John successfully builds trust and rapport with his team. This foundation of trust leads to honest discussions about challenges and more collaborative problem-solving, setting the department on a path to recovery and success.

Call to Action

1. **Plan a trust-building activity with a coachee (e.g., share a personal story or acknowledge a shared challenge).**

Your Notes:

_____

_____

_____

_____

_____

_____

_____

2. **Ask your coachee for feedback on your relationship and take actionable steps based on their input.**

Your Notes:

_____

_____

_____

_____

_____

_____

_____

Models and Techniques
Active Listening

- **Origin:** Popularized by Carl Rogers and Richard Farson in their work on client-centered therapy in the 1950s.
- **Usage:** Enhances communication and understanding between coach and coachee.
- **Description:** Active Listening involves fully concentrating on, understanding, responding to, and remembering what the coachee says. Techniques include maintaining eye contact, nodding, paraphrasing, summarizing, and asking open-ended questions.

Empathy

- **Origin:** The concept of empathy has been studied extensively by psychologists, including Carl Rogers.
- **Usage:** Strengthens the connection between coach and coachee by showing genuine care and understanding.
- **Description:** Empathy involves acknowledging and validating the coachee's feelings and experiences. Techniques include expressing understanding, showing concern, and offering support.

SBI Model (Situation-Behavior-Impact)

- **Origin:** Developed by the Center for Creative Leadership in the early 2000s.
- **Usage:** Used to provide clear, specific, and actionable feedback.
- **Description:** The SBI Model helps in delivering feedback by breaking it down into three components:
  - **Situation:** Describe the specific situation where the behavior occurred.
  - **Behavior:** Detail the observable behavior that occurred.
  - **Impact:** Explain the impact of the behavior on others, the team, or the organization.

Trust-Building Activities

- **Origin:** Various, common in team-building and leadership training.
- **Usage:** To create a foundation of trust and strong relationships between coach and coachee.
- **Description:** Activities that promote transparency, reliability, and personal connection. Examples include sharing personal stories, being open about intentions, and consistently following through on commitments.

By integrating these techniques and models into your coaching practice, you can build stronger, more effective relationships with your coachees. Trust and rapport are essential for creating a productive coaching environment where individuals feel valued, motivated, and equipped to achieve their goals. As you continue on your coaching journey, remember that building trust and rapport is an ongoing process that requires intention, consistency, and genuine care. Embrace these principles, and watch the transformative power they bring to your coaching relationships.

CHAPTER 3

The Power of Active Listening

"To listen well is as powerful a means of communication and influence as to talk well."

—John Marshall

A ctive listening is a powerful tool in the coach's arsenal. It involves fully concentrating, understanding, and responding thoughtfully to your coachee. This chapter will teach you the principles of active listening, techniques to improve your listening skills, and the benefits of truly hearing your coachee.

Understanding Active Listening

Active listening is more than just hearing words. It's about fully engaging with the speaker, understanding their message, and responding in a way that shows you have truly heard and understood them. This deep level of listening builds trust, fosters open communication, and creates a strong foundation for effective coaching.

Active listening is a fundamental skill in coaching, leadership, and personal relationships. It involves fully concentrating, understanding, and responding thoughtfully to what the other person is saying. This chapter will teach you the principles of active listening, techniques to improve your listening skills, and the benefits of truly hearing your coachee.

The Principles of Active Listening

Active listening goes beyond simply hearing words; it requires deep engagement with the speaker. Here are the core principles of active listening:

1. **Be Present:** Give the speaker your full attention. Avoid distractions and focus entirely on the conversation.

2. **Show Interest:** Demonstrate that you are engaged and interested in what the speaker is saying through non-verbal cues like nodding, maintaining eye contact, and leaning slightly forward.

3. **Avoid Interrupting:** Let the speaker finish their thoughts before you respond. Interrupting can make them feel unheard and undervalued.

4. **Reflect and Clarify:** Summarize what the speaker has said to ensure understanding and show that you are listening. Ask clarifying questions if needed.

5. **Empathize:** Try to understand the speaker's feelings and perspective. Show empathy by acknowledging their emotions and validating their experiences.

Techniques to Improve Your Listening Skills

Improving your listening skills takes practice and conscious effort. Here are some techniques to help you become a more effective listener:

1. **Paraphrasing**: Restate what the speaker has said in your own words. This not only shows that you are listening but also helps to confirm your understanding.
   ◦ Example: "So, what you're saying is that you're feeling overwhelmed by the new project deadlines, right?"
2. **Summarizing**: Provide a brief summary of the main points the speaker has made. This technique is especially useful in longer conversations.
   ◦ Example: "To summarize, you're concerned about the project timelines, the lack of resources, and the unclear expectations from the management."
3. **Reflective Listening**: Mirror the speaker's emotions and thoughts to show empathy and understanding.
   ◦ Example: "It sounds like you're really frustrated with the current situation. That must be difficult for you."
4. **Asking Open-Ended Questions**: Encourage the speaker to elaborate on their thoughts and feelings by asking questions that cannot be answered with a simple yes or no.
   ◦ Example: "Can you tell me more about what challenges you're facing with the new project?"
5. **Non-Verbal Cues**: Use body language to show that you are engaged. Maintain eye contact, nod, and use appropriate facial expressions to convey interest and understanding.
6. **Mindful Listening**: Practice mindfulness techniques to stay focused on the present moment. This helps prevent your mind from wandering and keeps you engaged in the conversation.

The Benefits of Truly Hearing Your Coachee

Active listening can have a profound impact on your coaching relationships. Here are some benefits of truly hearing your coachee:

1. **Builds Trust and Rapport:** When coachees feel heard and understood, they are more likely to trust you and open up about their challenges and aspirations.
2. **Enhances Understanding:** Active listening helps you gain a deeper understanding of your coachee's needs, goals, and concerns, enabling you to provide more effective guidance.
3. **Fosters Collaboration:** By actively listening, you create an environment of mutual respect and collaboration, where ideas can be freely exchanged and explored.
4. **Improves Problem-Solving:** Understanding your coachee's perspective allows you to identify the root causes of issues and develop more targeted solutions.
5. **Increases Engagement:** When coachees feel valued and heard, they are more likely to be engaged and committed to their development and the coaching process.

Applying Active Listening in Coaching

To effectively integrate active listening into your coaching practice, follow these steps:

1. **Prepare Mentally:** Before each coaching session, take a few moments to clear your mind and focus on being present.
2. **Set the Stage:** Create a conducive environment for open communication. Ensure privacy, minimize distractions, and make the coachee feel comfortable.
3. **Use Active Listening Techniques:** Throughout the conversation, employ techniques such as paraphrasing, summarizing, and asking open-ended questions.
4. **Reflect and Adjust:** After each session, reflect on your listening skills. Identify areas where you can improve and set goals for your next conversation.
5. **Seek Feedback:** Ask your coachee for feedback on your listening skills. Use their insights to enhance your ability to truly hear and understand them.

Scenario: Active Listening in Action

To illustrate the power of active listening, let's dive into a detailed scenario:

Stacy, a project manager, notices that one of her team members, Mike, is consistently missing deadlines. Instead of reprimanding him, she decides to practice active listening during their one-on-one meeting.

Setting the Stage: Stacy schedules a private meeting with Mike in a quiet, comfortable room. She ensures that there are no distractions, turning off her phone and closing her laptop.

Initial Conversation: Stacy: "Mike, I've noticed that you've been missing some deadlines lately, and I wanted to check in with you. How are things going for you?"

Active Listening Techniques:

- **Paraphrasing:** "So, what you're saying is that you're feeling overwhelmed by the new project deadlines, right?"
- **Summarizing:** "To summarize, you're concerned about the project timelines, the lack of resources, and the unclear expectations from the management."
- **Reflective Listening:** "It sounds like you're really frustrated with the current situation. That must be difficult for you."
- **Asking Open-Ended Questions:** "Can you tell me more about what challenges you're facing with the new project?"

Mike's Response: Mike opens up and shares that he is going through a tough time personally. His father has been ill, and he has been spending a lot of time caring for him. Additionally, he feels that the project timelines are unrealistic and that he hasn't received enough support from the team.

Empathy and Support: Stacy: "I'm really sorry to hear about your father, Mike. That sounds incredibly challenging. It's understandable that this would affect your work. Let's figure out a plan together to manage your workload better."

Collaborative Problem-Solving: Together, Stacy and Mike devise a plan to manage his workload more effectively. They decide to:
1. Prioritize tasks to focus on the most critical deadlines.
2. Reallocate some of Mike's tasks to other team members temporarily.
3. Schedule regular check-ins to monitor progress and provide additional support as needed.
4. Set more realistic timelines for the project based on the current team capacity.

Outcome: By practicing active listening, Stacy gains a deeper understanding of Mike's situation and challenges. This approach not only helps Mike feel heard and supported but also leads to a more effective and realistic project plan. As a result, Mike's performance improves, and the work environment becomes more supportive and collaborative.

Know Your Customers

Demonstrating empathy in your coaching relationships does more than just build trust and rapport—it also teaches empathy to your coachees. When you consistently model empathetic behavior, you provide a powerful example for your coachees to emulate. This not only enhances their personal development but also equips them with the skills they need to build strong, meaningful relationships with their customers.

Empathy is a cornerstone of effective customer relationships. By understanding and responding to the emotions, needs, and perspectives of others, your coachees can create more personalized and impactful interactions. As they observe and experience your empathetic approach, they learn how to listen deeply, ask the right questions, and offer genuine support. This ability to connect on a human level can transform their customer interactions, fostering loyalty and trust.

Encourage your coachees to practice empathy in their customer engagements. Teach them to actively listen to their customers, seeking to understand their challenges and aspirations. Show them how to respond with compassion and authenticity, offering solutions that truly meet their customers' needs. As they build these empathetic connections, they will not only improve customer satisfaction but also drive better business outcomes.

By demonstrating empathy, you are not just enhancing your coaching relationships—you are also empowering your coachees to know their customers better. This deeper understanding leads to more effective communication, stronger relationships, and ultimately, greater success. Empathy is a skill that ripples outward, positively impacting everyone it touches. As your coachees learn to incorporate empathy into their daily interactions, they will become more adept at building trust and creating value, both in their professional roles and beyond.

Call to Action

1. **Reflect on a Recent Conversation:** Think about a recent coaching conversation. How well did you listen? What could you have done differently to improve your listening skills?
2. **Practice Active Listening:** Choose one active listening technique to focus on in your next coaching session. Pay attention to how it impacts the conversation.
3. **Seek Feedback:** After your next coaching session, ask your coachee for feedback on your listening skills. Use their insights to make adjustments and improvements.

Practice

1. **Practice active listening techniques (e.g., paraphrasing, asking open-ended questions) in your next coaching session.**

Your Notes:

_____

_____

_____

_____

_____

_____

_____

_____

2. Record a coaching conversation (with permission) and review it to assess your listening skills.

Your Notes:

_____

_____

_____

_____

_____

_____

_____

Techniques and Models for Active Listening

Active Listening Techniques

- **Origin:** Popularized by Carl Rogers and Richard Farson in their work on client-centered therapy in the 1950s.
- **Usage:** Enhances communication and understanding between coach and coachee.
- **Description:** Active Listening involves fully concentrating on, understanding, responding to, and remembering what the coachee says. Techniques include maintaining eye contact,

nodding, paraphrasing, summarizing, and asking open-ended questions.

Reflective Listening
- **Origin:** Derived from Carl Rogers' client-centered therapy.
- **Usage:** Helps the coachee feel understood and validated.
- **Description:** Reflective Listening involves repeating back what the coachee has said, often in the form of a question, to show that you are actively processing their message and to encourage further elaboration.

Empathy
- **Origin:** The concept of empathy has been studied extensively by psychologists, including Carl Rogers.
- **Usage:** Strengthens the connection between coach and coachee by showing genuine care and understanding.
- **Description:** Empathy involves acknowledging and validating the coachee's feelings and experiences. Techniques include expressing understanding, showing concern, and offering support.

Open-Ended Questions
- **Origin:** Widely used in counseling, coaching, and therapy.
- **Usage:** Encourages deeper exploration and understanding of the coachee's thoughts and feelings.
- **Description:** Open-Ended Questions are questions that cannot be answered with a simple "yes" or "no." They typically begin with "what," "how," or "why" and prompt the coachee to elaborate on their thoughts and feelings.

The Listening Cycle
- **Origin:** Developed by John Stewart and Carole Logan in their book "Bridges Not Walls."
- **Usage:** Provides a structured approach to active listening.

- **Description:** The Listening Cycle involves five steps:
  - **Attend:** Give full attention to the coachee.
  - **Acknowledge:** Show that you are listening through verbal and non-verbal cues.
  - **Invite:** Encourage the coachee to share more.
  - **Summarize:** Restate key points to confirm understanding.
  - **Ask:** Pose questions to deepen understanding and explore further.

By incorporating these techniques and models into your coaching practice, you can become a more effective listener and create deeper, more meaningful connections with your coachees. Active listening is a skill that can be developed with practice and intention. As you continue to hone your listening abilities, you will see the transformative impact it has on your coaching relationships and the outcomes you achieve.

Part 2

Coaching Skill
(Focusing on Professional Development)

CHAPTER 4

Identifying Strengths and Weaknesses

"By understanding our strengths, we can amplify them; by acknowledging our weaknesses, we can learn to manage them."

—Adam Grant

Understanding the strengths and weaknesses of your coachee is crucial for effective coaching. This knowledge allows you to tailor your coaching strategies to leverage strengths and address weaknesses. In this chapter, you will learn various methods for identifying strengths and weaknesses, such as SWOT analysis and 360-degree feedback.

The Importance of Identifying Strengths and Weaknesses

Knowing the strengths and weaknesses of your coachee provides a clear picture of where they excel and where they need improvement. This understanding helps you to:

1. **Customize Coaching Plans:** Tailor your coaching strategies to suit the unique needs of each coachee.
2. **Maximize Potential:** Leverage strengths to boost confidence and performance.
3. **Address Development Areas:** Create targeted plans to overcome weaknesses.
4. **Enhance Self-Awareness:** Help coachees understand their own capabilities and limitations.

Techniques for Identifying Strengths and Weaknesses

SWOT Analysis

A SWOT analysis is a strategic planning tool used to identify Strengths, Weaknesses, Opportunities, and Threats. This technique can be adapted for coaching to provide a comprehensive view of a coachee's capabilities and areas for improvement.

How to Conduct a SWOT Analysis

1. **Strengths:** Identify internal attributes and resources that support achieving goals. Ask questions like:
   - What skills do you excel at?
   - What resources do you have access to?
   - What do others see as your strengths?
2. **Weaknesses:** Recognize internal attributes and resources that work against achieving goals. Consider:
   - What areas need improvement?
   - What skills are you lacking?
   - What do others see as your weaknesses?
3. **Opportunities:** Look for external factors that the coachee can leverage. Ask:
   - What opportunities are available to you?
   - How can you turn your strengths into opportunities?
4. **Threats:** Identify external factors that could cause trouble for the coachee. Consider:
   - What obstacles do you face?
   - What could hinder your progress?

Example: Alex's SWOT Analysis

Alex, an HR manager, is keen to understand and support a new team member, Lisa, who has shown promise but also faces some challenges. To get a comprehensive view of her strengths, weaknesses, opportunities, and threats, Alex decides to conduct a SWOT analysis.

Initial SWOT Analysis:

- **Strengths:** Lisa is recognized for her strategic thinking and excellent communication skills. She has a knack for seeing the big picture and articulating ideas clearly, making her a valuable asset in planning and presenting.
- **Weaknesses:** Lisa struggles with time management and handling stress, which occasionally impacts her ability to meet deadlines and maintain productivity.
- **Opportunities:** There are upcoming leadership training sessions that could enhance her management skills, as well as new project assignments that could provide her with more visibility and experience.
- **Threats:** Lisa is dealing with a heavy workload that could lead to potential burnout if not managed properly.

Personalized Development Plan: With these insights, Alex sits down with Lisa to discuss her SWOT analysis results. He appreciates her strengths and acknowledges how they contribute to the team's success. He also gently addresses her weaknesses, expressing his commitment to helping her improve.

Improving Time Management and Stress Handling: Alex suggests that Lisa attend a time management workshop and adopt tools like project management software to organize her tasks more effectively. He also recommends stress management techniques, such as mindfulness practices and regular breaks, to help her cope with her workload.

Leveraging Strengths in New Projects: To make the most of her strategic thinking and communication skills, Alex assigns Lisa to lead a new project that requires strategic planning and regular presentations to senior management. This will not only play to her strengths but also give her an opportunity to shine and grow.

Opportunities for Growth: Alex encourages Lisa to enroll in the upcoming leadership training sessions. These sessions are designed to build managerial skills and could be a great way for Lisa to prepare for future leadership roles. He also pairs her with a mentor who can provide guidance and support as she navigates her development plan.

Regular Check-ins: To ensure Lisa stays on track and feels supported, Alex schedules regular check-ins. During these meetings, they review her progress, celebrate her successes, and address any new challenges that arise. Alex remains proactive in adjusting the development plan as needed to keep it relevant and effective.

Outcome: With a clear and personalized development plan in place, Lisa begins to improve her time management and stress handling. She feels more confident and capable in her role, and her strategic thinking continues to benefit the team. The new project assignments allow her to demonstrate her strengths, and the leadership training prepares her for future opportunities.

By leveraging the SWOT analysis, Alex helps Lisa create a targeted development plan that addresses her weaknesses and capitalizes on her strengths, leading to professional growth and enhanced performance.

360-Degree Feedback

360-degree feedback involves gathering input from an employee's subordinates, peers, supervisors, and sometimes, external sources like customers. This comprehensive approach helps in understanding the employee's performance from different perspectives.

How to Implement 360-Degree Feedback

1. **Select Participants:** Choose a diverse group of people who interact regularly with the coachee.

2. **Create a Questionnaire:** Develop questions that cover various aspects of performance, such as communication, teamwork, and leadership.
3. **Collect Feedback:** Ensure anonymity to encourage honest and constructive feedback.
4. **Analyze Results:** Look for common themes and significant insights.
5. **Discuss Findings:** Share the feedback with the coachee, focusing on both strengths and areas for improvement.

Example: Maria's 360-Degree Feedback

Maria, a seasoned sales coach, recognizes the potential in David, a promising but inexperienced sales representative. To gain a comprehensive understanding of his performance, Maria decides to use 360-degree feedback. This method involves gathering feedback from various sources, including David's peers, supervisors, and clients.

360-Degree Feedback Summary:

- **Strengths:** The feedback highlights David's strong presentation skills and his ability to build good rapport with customers. His charisma and communication prowess make him a favorite among clients.
- **Weaknesses:** The feedback also points out David's inconsistent follow-up practices and the need for improvement in his time management skills. These weaknesses are impacting his ability to close deals and manage his workload effectively.

Personalized Development Plan: Armed with this detailed feedback, Maria schedules a one-on-one meeting with David to discuss the results. She starts by acknowledging his strengths, emphasizing how his presentation skills and customer rapport are valuable assets to the team.

Enhancing Follow-Up Practices: Maria and David brainstorm strategies to improve his follow-up practices. They decide to implement a structured follow-up schedule using a CRM system. Maria introduces David to specific tools and techniques for tracking customer interactions and setting reminders for follow-up actions. She also provides examples of effective follow-up emails and calls, helping David understand how to maintain consistent and meaningful communication with clients.

Improving Time Management: To address his time management issues, Maria suggests time management techniques such as the Pomodoro Technique and the Eisenhower Matrix. They set up a weekly planning session where David can prioritize tasks, allocate time slots for different activities, and set achievable daily goals. Maria also recommends using calendar alerts and task management apps to keep David on track.

Leveraging Strengths: While focusing on improvement areas, Maria encourages David to continue leveraging his strong presentation skills and customer relationships. She assigns him to lead more client presentations and product demos, allowing him to shine and build confidence. Maria also pairs David with a mentor who excels in follow-up and time management, providing him with additional support and guidance.

Regular Check-ins: Maria schedules regular check-ins with David to monitor his progress. During these meetings, they review his follow-up practices, time management strategies, and overall performance. Maria provides ongoing feedback and adjusts the development plan as necessary to ensure it remains effective and relevant.

Outcome: With a clear development plan and consistent support from Maria, David starts to improve his follow-up practices and time management skills. His structured approach to follow-ups leads to better client relationships and more closed deals. By managing his time more effectively, David becomes more productive and less stressed.

David's enhanced skills, combined with his natural strengths in presentation and customer rapport, contribute to his overall success as a sales representative. Maria's use of 360-degree feedback and her tailored coaching plan help David reach his potential and excel in his role.

By leveraging the comprehensive insights from 360-degree feedback, Maria helps David create a targeted development plan that addresses his weaknesses while building on his strengths, leading to significant professional growth and improved performance.

Tailoring Coaching Strategies

Once you have identified the strengths and weaknesses of your coachee, you can tailor your coaching strategies to meet their specific needs.

Leveraging Strengths

1. **Build Confidence:** Encourage coachees to use their strengths in challenging situations to boost their confidence.
2. **Assign Relevant Tasks:** Give tasks that align with their strengths to maximize efficiency and satisfaction.
3. **Recognition:** Acknowledge and celebrate their strengths to reinforce positive behavior.

Addressing Weaknesses

1. **Set Development Goals:** Create specific, measurable goals to address areas of weakness.
2. **Provide Resources:** Offer training, tools, and resources to help improve weak areas.
3. **Regular Check-Ins:** Monitor progress regularly and adjust plans as needed.

Call to Action

1. Conduct a SWOT analysis for one of your coachees to identify their strengths and weaknesses.

Your Notes:

_____

_____

_____

_____

_____

2. Implement a 360-degree feedback process and discuss the results with your coachee.

Your Notes:

_____

_____

_____

_____

_____

Techniques and Models for Identifying Strengths and Weaknesses

SWOT Analysis

- **Origin:** Developed by Albert Humphrey in the 1960s at the Stanford Research Institute.
- **Usage:** To assess internal strengths and weaknesses, and external opportunities and threats.
- **Description:** SWOT Analysis is a strategic planning tool that helps in identifying the internal and external factors that are

favorable or unfavorable to achieving an objective. It involves creating a matrix with four quadrants: Strengths, Weaknesses, Opportunities, and Threats.

Strengths	Weaknesses
Opportunities	Threats

360-Degree Feedback

- **Origin:** Concept emerged in the 1950s, widely adopted in the 1990s.
- **Usage:** To gather comprehensive feedback from multiple sources.
- **Description:** 360-Degree Feedback involves collecting feedback from an employee's subordinates, peers, supervisors, and sometimes, external sources like customers. This holistic approach helps in understanding the employee's performance from different perspectives.

By incorporating these techniques into your coaching practice, you can gain a deeper understanding of your coachee's strengths and weaknesses. This insight allows you to provide more effective, tailored coaching that helps your coachee reach their full potential. Remember, the goal is to create a balanced approach that leverages strengths while addressing areas for improvement, fostering a well-rounded and confident individual.

CHAPTER 5

Tailoring Development Plans

"One-size-fits-all approaches do not work. Personal development plans should be tailored to the individual to bring out the best in each person."

—Richard Branson

Creating personalized development plans is essential for fostering professional growth. These plans should be tailored to address the specific needs and goals of your coachee. In this chapter, you will learn how to design and implement development plans using techniques like SMART goals and Individual Development Plans (IDPs).

The Importance of Personalized Development Plans

Personalized development plans are crucial for several reasons:

1. **Focus on Individual Needs:** Tailoring plans to individual coachees ensures that their unique strengths, weaknesses, and career aspirations are addressed.

2. **Motivation and Engagement:** Coachees are more likely to be motivated and engaged when they see that their development is taken seriously and aligned with their personal goals.

3. **Measurable Progress:** Structured plans allow for tracking progress and making necessary adjustments, ensuring continuous improvement.

4. **Accountability:** Clear development plans create accountability for both the coach and the coachee, fostering a sense of responsibility and commitment.

Designing Personalized Development Plans

Setting SMART Goals

One technique that I have used and trained on over and over again in my career is SMART goals. If you happen to come across my other books or any articles I have written or seen me speak at a conference or on a podcast, you likely heard me reference SMART goals. I believe it is easy to verbalize a goal, but elevating that goal to a SMART goal using the framework below exponentially increases the likelihood of achieving it. SMART goals are a powerful tool for creating clear, actionable objectives. SMART stands for Specific, Measurable, Achievable, Relevant, and Time-bound.

How to Set SMART Goals

1. **Specific:** Clearly define what you want to achieve.
   - Example: "Increase sales by 15% in the next quarter."
2. **Measurable:** Establish criteria for measuring progress.
   - Example: "Track weekly sales metrics to ensure we're on target."
3. **Achievable:** Ensure the goal is realistic and attainable.
   - Example: "Based on last quarter's performance, a 15% increase is challenging but achievable."
4. **Relevant:** Align the goal with broader organizational objectives.
   - Example: "Increasing sales aligns with our company's growth strategy."
5. **Time-bound:** Set a deadline for achieving the goal.
   - Example: "Achieve this by the end of the next quarter."

SMART GOALS TEMPLATE

S	Specific	• Who is involved? • What do I want to achieve? • When do I need to achieve this? • Why is the goal important?	
M	Measurable	• How will I measure my progress? • How will I know if my goal is achieved?	
A	Achievable	• Will it be clear when the goal is complete? • Is it reasonable to complete the goal in the time allotted?	
R	Relevant	• Is this goal related to my overall success (or the success of my business/organization)	
T	Time-Bound	• How long should it take to accomplish this goal? • When will I check in on whether or not the goal has been completed? • Am I ready to start work on the goal?	

Example: David's SMART Goals

David, a motivated sales representative, is eager to boost his performance and contribute more significantly to the company's revenue goals. Together, we set a series of SMART goals to provide him with a clear, structured path to achieve these aspirations.

SMART Goals:

- **Specific:** Increase the number of client meetings by 20% each month.
- **Measurable:** Use CRM software to accurately track and record the number of client meetings.
- **Achievable:** Considering David's current performance metrics, this goal is challenging but realistic with improved time management and effort.
- **Relevant:** Increasing client meetings is directly aligned with the company's revenue objectives, as more meetings typically translate to more sales opportunities.

- **Time-bound:** This goal is set to be achieved by the end of the next quarter.

Detailed Plan to Achieve SMART Goals:

1. **Increase Client Meetings by 20% Each Month**
   - **Current Performance Analysis:** We start by reviewing David's current client meeting schedule. On average, he holds 15 client meetings per month.
   - **Target:** With a 20% increase, the goal is to reach 18 client meetings per month initially, then progressively increase each month.

2. **Use CRM Software to Track Meetings**
   - **CRM Integration:** David will leverage the company's CRM software to log every client meeting. This will not only track the number of meetings but also help analyze meeting outcomes and follow-up actions.
   - **Training:** We ensure David is fully trained on using the CRM software efficiently. This includes setting reminders, updating client interactions, and generating reports to monitor progress.

3. **Achievable with Proper Time Management**
   - **Time Management Techniques:** We implement time management techniques such as the Pomodoro Technique to help David focus on scheduling and preparing for client meetings. Additionally, we use the Eisenhower Matrix to prioritize tasks, ensuring that scheduling client meetings remains a top priority.
   - **Weekly Planning:** David will set aside time at the beginning of each week to plan his client outreach and meeting schedule. This dedicated planning time will help ensure he consistently meets his monthly targets.

4. **Aligning with Company's Revenue Goals**
   - **Revenue Alignment:** Increasing client meetings should logically lead to more sales opportunities. We discuss the correlation between meeting frequency and sales conversions to reinforce the relevance of this goal.
   - **Sales Training:** David participates in sales training sessions focused on converting client meetings into sales. This helps ensure that the increased number of meetings directly contributes to higher sales figures.
5. **Achieving by the End of the Next Quarter**
   - **Quarterly Timeline:** We break down the quarterly goal into monthly milestones. For example, if David starts with 15 meetings in the first month, the target is 18 meetings, followed by 22, and so on.
   - **Progress Check-ins:** We schedule bi-weekly check-ins to review David's progress, address any challenges, and adjust strategies as needed. This regular review helps keep David accountable and motivated.

Outcome: With these SMART goals in place, David begins to see a structured path toward improving his performance. The clear, measurable objectives provide him with a tangible target to aim for each month. The use of CRM software helps him stay organized and track his progress, while time management techniques ensure he can effectively balance his workload.

By the end of the quarter, David's dedication and strategic planning result in a significant increase in client meetings. This not only boosts his sales figures but also enhances his confidence and skills as a sales representative. The incremental success each month keeps him motivated and engaged, ultimately contributing to the overall success of the sales team and the company's revenue goals.

Creating Individual Development Plans (IDPs)

An Individual Development Plan (IDP) is a personalized, actionable plan designed to help coachees achieve their professional goals.

Components of an IDP

1. **Personal Information:** Basic details about the coachee.
2. **Career Goals:** Short-term and long-term career aspirations.
3. **Current Skills and Competencies:** Assessment of current skills and areas for improvement.
4. **Development Objectives:** Specific objectives that align with career goals.
5. **Action Plan:** Detailed steps to achieve development objectives, including resources and support needed.
6. **Timeline:** Deadlines for each step in the action plan.
7. **Monitoring and Evaluation:** Regular check-ins to review progress and make necessary adjustments.

Example: Lila's IDP

Lila, a dedicated marketing associate, is eager to advance her career and take on more leadership responsibilities. Together, we crafted a comprehensive Individual Development Plan (IDP) to guide her professional growth and help her achieve her career goals.

Individual Development Plan (IDP) for Liia:

Career Goals:
- **Objective:** Become a marketing manager within three years.

Current Skills and Competencies:
- **Strengths:** Strong in digital marketing, excellent analytical skills, and creative thinking.
- **Areas for Improvement:** Needs to enhance team leadership and gain experience in project management.

Development Objectives:

1. **Enhance Leadership Skills**
   - **Training and Mentorship:** Enroll in leadership training programs and seek mentorship from experienced leaders within the organization.
   - **Target:** Develop a deeper understanding of effective leadership practices and build confidence in leading a team.

2. **Gain Experience in Project Management**
   - **Project Involvement:** Take on roles that involve managing marketing projects, from planning to execution.
   - **Target:** Gain hands-on experience in project management to enhance organizational and leadership abilities.

Action Plan:

1. **Enroll in a Leadership Training Program**
   - **Timeline:** Within the next month.
   - **Details:** Research and select a leadership training program that focuses on essential leadership skills such as communication, conflict resolution, and team motivation.
   - **Execution:** Enroll in the program and actively participate in all training sessions.

2. **Take on a Project Management Role**
   - **Timeline:** For the upcoming marketing campaign, within the next quarter.
   - **Details:** Assume the role of project manager for the next major marketing campaign. This involves planning, coordinating, and overseeing the campaign from start to finish.
   - **Execution:** Work closely with the marketing team to ensure successful project delivery, while applying newly learned leadership skills.

Timeline:

- **Leadership Training:** Complete within six months.
- **Project Management Role:** Lead a project team within the next quarter.

Monitoring and Evaluation:

1. **Monthly Check-ins**
   - **Frequency:** Monthly.
   - **Details:** Schedule regular one-on-one meetings to discuss Lila's progress, challenges, and any support she may need.
   - **Execution:** Use these check-ins to provide feedback, review accomplishments, and adjust the action plan as necessary.
2. **Feedback and Performance Review**
   - **Frequency:** Quarterly reviews.
   - **Details:** Conduct in-depth evaluations of Lila's performance in her new roles and responsibilities.
   - **Execution:** Provide constructive feedback and recognition for her achievements, and identify any additional areas for development.

Outcome: With this IDP in place, Lila has a clear roadmap for achieving her career goals. The structured plan allows her to systematically develop the skills and experience needed to become a marketing manager.

Detailed Scenario Execution:

1. **Leadership Training Enrollment:** Lila begins by researching various leadership training programs and selects one that offers a comprehensive curriculum on essential leadership skills. She enrolls in the program and commits to attending all sessions, eager to absorb as much knowledge as possible.
2. **Project Management Role:** As the next major marketing campaign approaches, Lila takes on the role of project manager. She starts by organizing a kickoff meeting, clearly defining

the campaign's goals, and delegating tasks to team members. Throughout the project, Lila applies the leadership principles she's learning, fostering a collaborative and motivated team environment.

3. **Monthly Check-ins:** In our monthly check-ins, we discuss Lila's progress. She shares insights from her leadership training and how she's applying them in her project management role. We address any challenges she faces, such as managing team dynamics or handling unexpected project hurdles, and brainstorm solutions together.

4. **Feedback and Performance Review:** At the end of each quarter, we conduct a thorough performance review. Lila's efforts in leading the project team and her growth in leadership skills are recognized and celebrated. Constructive feedback is provided, highlighting areas for further improvement and setting new targets for the next quarter.

Results: Over the six-month period, Lila completes her leadership training and successfully manages the marketing campaign. Her newfound leadership skills and project management experience significantly boost her confidence and competence. By the end of the next quarter, Lila is well on her way to achieving her goal of becoming a marketing manager, demonstrating her potential to take on even greater responsibilities within the organization.

Conclusion: The detailed IDP not only guides Lila's professional development but also ensures she receives the necessary support and feedback throughout her journey. By focusing on tailored development objectives, actionable plans, and regular evaluations, Lila is empowered to unlock her full potential and achieve her career aspirations.

Implementing Development Plans

Once the development plan is created, it's crucial to implement it effectively. Here are some strategies:

1. **Regular Check-Ins:** Schedule regular meetings to discuss progress, address challenges, and adjust the plan as necessary.
2. **Provide Resources:** Ensure the coachee has access to the necessary resources, such as training programs, mentorship, and tools.
3. **Celebrate Milestones:** Recognize and celebrate achievements to maintain motivation and momentum.
4. **Adjust as Needed:** Be flexible and open to making adjustments to the plan based on feedback and changing circumstances.

Call to Action

1. Work with a coachee to set three SMART goals related to their professional development.

Your Notes:

_____

_____

_____

_____

_____

_____

2. Draft an Individual Development Plan (IDP) for one of your coachees, including career goals, development objectives, and an action plan.

Your Notes:

_____

_____

_____

_____

_____

_____

_____

Techniques and Models for Tailoring Development Plans

SMART Goals

- **Origin:** First mentioned by George T. Doran in 1981.
- **Usage:** To create clear and achievable goals.
- **Description:** SMART is a mnemonic acronym, giving criteria to guide in the setting of objectives. It stands for Specific, Measurable, Achievable, Relevant, and Time-bound. Each element of the SMART framework works together to create a goal that is carefully planned and trackable.

Individual Development Plans (IDPs)

- **Origin:** Widely used in career development since the 1980s.
- **Usage:** To outline the personal and professional development of an individual.
- **Description:** IDPs are customized plans created in collaboration between the employee and their manager or coach, focusing on specific areas for development. They include goals, required skills, competencies, and action steps.

By incorporating these techniques into your coaching practice, you can create personalized development plans that effectively foster professional growth. These plans provide a structured and targeted approach to development, helping your coachees achieve their career aspirations while contributing to the success of your organization. Remember, the goal is to create a balanced approach that addresses the unique needs of each coachee, fostering a well-rounded and confident individual ready to excel in their career.

CHAPTER 6

Providing Constructive Feedback

"Criticism, like rain, should be gentle enough to nourish a man's
growth without destroying his roots."

—Frank A. Clark

Feedback is a critical component of the coaching process, but it must
be delivered constructively to be effective. This chapter will guide
you on how to provide feedback that is clear, specific, and actionable
using frameworks like the SBI (Situation-Behavior-Impact) model.

The Importance of Constructive Feedback

Constructive feedback is essential for several reasons:

1. **Clarity:** Clear feedback helps coachees understand what they
   are doing well and where they need to improve.
2. **Growth:** Constructive feedback encourages continuous learning and development.
3. **Motivation:** When delivered effectively, feedback can motivate
   coachees to strive for excellence.
4. **Trust:** Providing honest and respectful feedback builds trust
   and strengthens the coaching relationship.

Principles of Constructive Feedback

Be Specific

General feedback can be confusing and unhelpful. Specific feedback pin-
points exact behaviors and outcomes, making it easier for coachees to
understand and act on.

Example:

- Instead of saying, "Good job on the presentation," say, "Your presentation was well-organized, and the way you highlighted the key data points kept the audience engaged."

Focus on Behavior, Not the Person

Feedback should address specific behaviors and their impact, not personal characteristics. This approach helps coachees see that their actions, not their inherent traits, are the focus.

Example:

- Instead of saying, "You're not a good listener," say, "I noticed during meetings that you often interrupt others, which can make it difficult for team members to share their ideas."

Be Timely

Provide feedback as soon as possible after the behavior or event. Timely feedback is more relevant and easier for the coachee to connect to their actions.

Example:

- Instead of waiting until the end of the month, give feedback immediately after a project presentation or a meeting.

Balance Positive and Negative Feedback

While it's essential to address areas for improvement, balancing this with positive feedback helps maintain motivation and morale.

Example:

- Highlight what the coachee did well before addressing areas for improvement. This approach shows appreciation for their efforts while guiding them towards better performance.

The SBI (Situation-Behavior-Impact) Model

When it comes to delivering feedback, the SBI model is a powerful framework that is clear, specific, and actionable. If you have ever taken a "management course" you have likely come across the SBI Model. It helps structure feedback by breaking it down into three components: Situation, Behavior, and Impact.

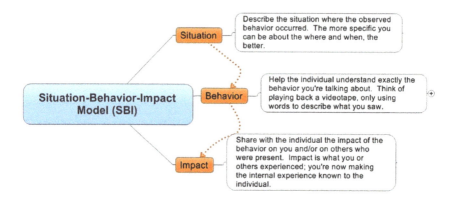

How to Use the SBI Model

1. **Situation:** Describe the specific situation where the behavior occurred.
   - Example: "During yesterday's team meeting..."
2. **Behavior:** Detail the observable behavior that occurred.
   - Example: "You interrupted Sarah several times while she was presenting her ideas..."
3. **Impact:** Explain the impact of the behavior on others, the team, or the organization.
   - Example: "This made it difficult for her to convey her points and affected the team's ability to discuss her ideas effectively."

Scenario: Using SBI for Positive Feedback

Example:

Situation: "In the client presentation last Friday..."

- **Specific Context:** Last Friday, we had an important presentation with a potential client where you were one of the key presenters.

Behavior: "You clearly explained our product's benefits and addressed the client's concerns with detailed answers..."

- **Detailed Observation:** During the presentation, you effectively highlighted the unique benefits of our product. Additionally, when the client raised concerns, you responded with thorough and well-prepared answers, demonstrating a deep understanding of their needs.

Impact: "This helped build the client's confidence in our solutions and contributed to closing the deal."

- **Result of the Behavior:** Your clarity and preparedness significantly boosted the client's confidence in our solutions. As a result, they felt assured about our capability to meet their needs, which played a crucial role in their decision to move forward with the deal.

Detailed Scenario Execution:

Preparation for Feedback: In preparing to deliver this feedback, I make sure to gather all the specifics about the situation, observe the exact behavior, and understand the impact it had on the client and our business.

During the Feedback Session:

- I start by setting a positive tone and thanking the team member for their efforts.
- **Situation:** I clearly state the context of the feedback: "In the client presentation last Friday, we were in a critical phase of securing a new client."

- **Behavior:** I then describe their specific actions: "You clearly explained our product's benefits and addressed the client's concerns with detailed answers."
- **Impact:** Finally, I outline the positive result: "This helped build the client's confidence in our solutions and contributed to closing the deal."

Follow-Up:
- I encourage the team member to continue this behavior and discuss how they can further leverage their strengths in future presentations.
- We also brainstorm any additional support or resources they might need to keep excelling in client interactions.

Scenario: Using SBI for Developmental Feedback
Example:
Situation: "During the team brainstorming session on Monday..."
- **Specific Context:** This feedback relates to our team brainstorming session that took place on Monday, where collaboration and idea-sharing were the main goals.

Behavior: "You often cut off your colleagues mid-sentence..."
- **Detailed Observation:** Throughout the session, I noticed that you frequently interrupted your colleagues while they were speaking. This behavior was observed multiple times, hindering the flow of the discussion.

Impact: "This discouraged them from sharing their ideas and affected the collaborative spirit of the session."
- **Result of the Behavior:** These interruptions discouraged some team members from contributing their ideas and negatively impacted the collaborative environment we aim to foster. It

created a sense of hesitation among the team, reducing the overall effectiveness of the session.

Detailed Scenario Execution:

Preparation for Feedback: Before delivering this feedback, I ensure I have clear examples of the behavior and its impact. I also consider how to frame the feedback constructively to support the team member's growth.

During the Feedback Session:
- I start by expressing the importance of the team member's contributions and my commitment to their development.
- **Situation:** I clearly define the context: "During the team brainstorming session on Monday, where we were generating ideas for the new project."
- **Behavior:** I describe the specific behavior: "You often cut off your colleagues mid-sentence."
- **Impact:** I explain the consequence: "This discouraged them from sharing their ideas and affected the collaborative spirit of the session."

Follow-Up:
- We discuss strategies to improve, such as actively listening, waiting for colleagues to finish speaking, and using non-verbal cues to indicate readiness to contribute.
- I offer support through resources or training on communication skills if needed.
- We set a follow-up meeting to review progress and discuss any challenges they might face in implementing these changes.

Conclusion: Using the SBI model for both positive and developmental feedback helps ensure that feedback is clear, specific, and actionable. It encourages open communication, supports growth, and fosters a more productive and collaborative work environment.

Techniques for Providing Constructive Feedback

The Feedback Sandwich

The Feedback Sandwich was one of Priscilla's favorites and I was often on the receiving end of it. This technique involves structuring feedback by placing constructive criticism between positive comments. This approach helps make the feedback more palatable and maintains the coachee's motivation.

Example: The Feedback Sandwich

Positive Comment: "Your report was very thorough and well-researched."
- **Context:** I acknowledge the effort and depth of the work done by the team member, emphasizing the comprehensive nature of their research.

Constructive Feedback: "However, I noticed that the formatting was inconsistent, which made it a bit hard to follow in some sections."
- **Observation:** I point out a specific area for improvement, detailing how the inconsistency in formatting affected the readability of the report.

Positive Comment: "Overall, your attention to detail is impressive, and with some tweaks to the formatting, it will be even more effective."
- **Encouragement:** I end on a positive note, reinforcing the team member's strengths and expressing confidence that addressing the formatting issue will enhance the report's overall impact.

Detailed Scenario Execution:

Preparation for Feedback: Before the feedback session, I review the report thoroughly to understand its strengths and areas needing improvement. I also prepare specific examples to illustrate my points.

During the Feedback Session:

- **Positive Comment:** I start the conversation with a genuine positive observation to set a constructive tone: "Your report was very thorough and well-researched. The depth of analysis and the quality of the data you presented were impressive."
- **Constructive Feedback:** I then provide clear, specific feedback on the area that needs improvement: "However, I noticed that the formatting was inconsistent in some sections. For example, the headings and bullet points varied, which made it a bit hard to follow the flow of information."
- **Positive Comment:** I conclude with another positive comment to maintain the team member's motivation and reinforce their strengths: "Overall, your attention to detail is impressive. With some tweaks to the formatting, such as standardizing headings and bullet points, your report will be even more effective and easier to navigate."

Follow-Up:

- I offer assistance or resources, such as templates or guidelines, to help improve the formatting.
- We discuss a timeline for revising the report and agree on a follow-up meeting to review the changes.
- I encourage the team member to ask for feedback on the formatting before the final submission to ensure consistency and clarity.

Conclusion: The Feedback Sandwich technique is an effective way to deliver constructive feedback while maintaining a positive and encouraging tone. By starting and ending with positive comments, the feedback becomes more palatable and motivates the team member to improve without feeling discouraged. This method fosters a supportive and collaborative work environment where continuous improvement is encouraged and recognized.

Encouraging Self-Reflection

Encouraging coachees to reflect on their performance can lead to valuable insights and self-directed improvement.

Example Questions:
1. "How do you feel the presentation went?"
2. "What do you think you did well?"
3. "Is there anything you would do differently next time?"

Detailed Scenario Execution:

Preparation for the Reflection Session: Before the session, I review the presentation thoroughly, noting key points, successes, and areas where there might have been challenges. I prepare the reflection questions to guide the team member through a thoughtful analysis of their performance.

During the Reflection Session:
1. **"How do you feel the presentation went?"**
   - **Opening the Conversation:** I start with an open-ended question that invites the team member to share their overall impressions and feelings about their presentation. This helps them to relax and begin thinking critically about their experience.
   - **Example:** "Mike, now that you've had some time to reflect, how do you feel the presentation went yesterday? What are your initial thoughts and feelings?"
2. **"What do you think you did well?"**
   - **Positive Reinforcement:** I encourage the team member to identify and articulate their strengths and successes during the presentation. This builds their confidence and helps them recognize their achievements.
   - **Example:** "Let's focus on what went well. What do you think were your strong points during the presentation? What aspects are you most proud of?"

3. **"Is there anything you would do differently next time?"**
   - **Constructive Self-Critique:** I guide the team member to consider areas for improvement, fostering a mindset of continuous learning and development. This helps them think about actionable changes for future presentations.
   - **Example:** "Reflecting on the presentation, is there anything you would do differently next time? Are there specific areas where you feel you could improve or approach things differently?"

Follow-Up:
   - **Developing Action Plans:** Based on the team member's reflections, we discuss specific actions they can take to build on their strengths and address areas for improvement. This might include additional training, practice sessions, or seeking feedback from colleagues.
   - **Setting Goals:** We set clear, achievable goals for their next presentation, incorporating their reflections to ensure they are continuously developing their skills.
   - **Ongoing Support:** I offer my support and resources to help them achieve these goals, emphasizing that self-reflection is an ongoing process that contributes to their professional growth.

Conclusion: The self-reflection technique empowers team members to critically evaluate their performance and take ownership of their development. By asking thoughtful, open-ended questions, I encourage them to recognize their successes and identify areas for improvement. This method not only enhances their self-awareness and confidence but also fosters a culture of continuous learning and growth. Encouraging regular self-reflection helps team members to develop a proactive approach to their professional development and equips them with the skills to continuously improve and excel in their roles.

Creating an Action Plan

After providing feedback, work with your coachee to create an action plan for addressing areas of improvement. This plan should include specific steps, resources needed, and a timeline.

Detailed Scenario Execution:

Feedback Session Preparation: Before the session, review the coachee's recent work and gather specific examples to provide clear and actionable feedback. Prepare to discuss the feedback constructively and collaboratively develop an action plan.

During the Feedback Session:
Providing Feedback:

- **Clear and Specific Feedback:** Deliver the feedback in a clear, specific, and constructive manner. Use the Situation-Behavior-Impact (SBI) model to structure the feedback.
- **Example Feedback:** "In your recent reports, the content is very detailed and thorough, which is excellent. However, I've noticed that the formatting is inconsistent, which makes it a bit difficult to follow in some sections."

Collaborative Action Plan Development:
Step 1: Review Guidelines for Consistent Formatting

- **Identify Resources:** Discuss the resources needed to address the formatting issues, such as company guidelines, templates, or examples of well-formatted reports.
- **Example Conversation:** "Let's start by reviewing the company's guidelines for report formatting. I'll share the document with you, and we can go through it together to ensure you understand the expectations."

Step 2: Implement These Guidelines in the Next Report
- **Practical Application:** Plan how to apply the guidelines in the coachee's next piece of work. Offer support and resources to help them implement these changes effectively.
- **Example Conversation:** "For your next report, I'd like you to implement these formatting guidelines. If you have any questions or need assistance while working on it, feel free to reach out to me."

Step 3: Schedule a Review Session to Assess Improvements
- **Set a Timeline:** Establish a timeline for completing the steps and schedule a follow-up meeting to review the updated report.
- **Example Conversation:** "Let's schedule a review session for next week, where we can go over your next report together. This will give us the opportunity to assess the improvements and discuss any further refinements."

Follow-Up:
Regular Check-Ins:
- **Continuous Support:** Schedule regular check-ins to monitor progress and provide ongoing support. Ensure the coachee feels supported and encouraged throughout the process.
- **Example Conversation:** "I'll check in with you mid-week to see how things are progressing. If you encounter any challenges, we can address them together."

Feedback on Improvements:
- **Acknowledge Progress:** During the review session, acknowledge the coachee's efforts and progress. Provide additional feedback and guidance as needed.
- **Example Conversation:** "I see you've made significant improvements in the formatting of this report. It's much easier to follow. Let's continue to refine these skills and maintain this consistency in future reports."

Conclusion: The action plan technique empowers coachees to take concrete steps toward improvement by providing them with clear, structured guidance and support. By working collaboratively to develop an action plan, you ensure that the coachee understands the feedback and knows exactly how to address it. This approach not only fosters a sense of ownership and accountability but also builds confidence as they see their progress over time. Encouraging regular follow-ups and check-ins reinforces the importance of continuous improvement and helps maintain momentum toward achieving their development goals.

Example: Creating an Action Plan After Providing Feedback

Feedback: "Your reports are detailed but sometimes difficult to follow due to formatting issues."

Action Plan:

Step 1: Review Guidelines for Consistent Formatting

- **Identify Resources:** Discuss the resources needed to address the formatting issues, such as company guidelines, templates, or examples of well-formatted reports.
- **Example:** "Let's start by reviewing the company's guidelines for report formatting. I'll share the document with you, and we can go through it together to ensure you understand the expectations."

Step 2: Implement These Guidelines in the Next Report

- **Practical Application:** Plan how to apply the guidelines in the coachee's next piece of work. Offer support and resources to help them implement these changes effectively.
- **Example:** "For your next report, I'd like you to implement these formatting guidelines. If you have any questions or need assistance while working on it, feel free to reach out to me."

Step 3: Schedule a Review Session to Assess Improvements

- **Set a Timeline:** Establish a timeline for completing the steps and schedule a follow-up meeting to review the updated report.
- **Example:** "Let's schedule a review session for next week, where we can go over your next report together. This will give us the opportunity to assess the improvements and discuss any further refinements."

Follow-Up:

Regular Check-Ins:

- **Continuous Support:** Schedule regular check-ins to monitor progress and provide ongoing support. Ensure the coachee feels supported and encouraged throughout the process.
- **Example:** "I'll check in with you mid-week to see how things are progressing. If you encounter any challenges, we can address them together."

Feedback on Improvements:

- **Acknowledge Progress:** During the review session, acknowledge the coachee's efforts and progress. Provide additional feedback and guidance as needed.
- **Example:** "I see you've made significant improvements in the formatting of this report. It's much easier to follow. Let's continue to refine these skills and maintain this consistency in future reports."

Know Your Products

Coaching your coachees to develop their skills and knowledge does more than enhance their individual performance—it also instills a deep understanding of your products or services, empowering them to become true experts in what they sell. By fostering this expertise, you equip your coachees with the tools they need to communicate value effectively and build credibility with their customers.

Coaching to skill is not just about knowing your products but understanding how to effectively sell them. It requires honing the ability to uncover customer needs and create a compelling case for why your product will significantly enhance their experience. This involves developing deep product knowledge, mastering the art of storytelling, and employing strategic questioning techniques (deep discovery) to identify pain points and opportunities. By doing so, coachees can present not only the features and benefits of the product but also weave these into a narrative that resonates with the customer's unique situation. Demonstrating how your product can solve specific problems and deliver tangible value leads to stronger customer relationships and increased sales success.

When your coachees have a thorough grasp of the products or services they represent, they can confidently address customer needs, answer questions, and overcome objections. This knowledge allows them to tailor their sales approach to highlight the features and benefits most relevant to each customer. As you coach them to build their skills, you also teach them the importance of continuous learning and staying up-to-date with product developments and industry trends.

Encourage your coachees to dive deep into the details of what they are selling. Provide them with opportunities to engage with product experts, participate in training sessions, and explore real-world applications of the products or services. Use hands-on exercises, role-playing scenarios, and case studies to help them internalize this knowledge. By making skill development an ongoing process, you ensure that your coachees remain agile and adaptable in a constantly evolving marketplace.

As your coachees become more knowledgeable about your products, they will also learn to communicate this expertise in a way that resonates with customers. Teach them how to present information clearly and persuasively, focusing on the specific needs and pain points of their audience. This ability to articulate the value of your offerings is crucial for building trust and driving sales.

By coaching your coachees to know their products inside and out, you are not just enhancing their capabilities—you are empowering them to become trusted advisors to their customers. This deep product knowledge, combined with effective communication skills, positions them to deliver exceptional customer experiences and drive meaningful business results. Knowing what you sell is not just about having the facts; it's about using that knowledge to create lasting, impactful relationships with your customers.

Call to Action

1. Use the SBI model to prepare for your next feedback session.

Your Notes:

_____

_____

_____

_____

_____

_____

_____

2. Deliver feedback to a coachee and ask for their thoughts on its effectiveness.

Your Notes:

_____

_____

_____

_____

_____

_____

_____

3. Encourage self-reflection by asking your coachee to evaluate their own performance.

Your Notes:

_____

_____

_____

_____

_____

_____

Techniques and Models for Providing Constructive Feedback

SBI Model (Situation-Behavior-Impact)
- **Origin:** Developed by the Center for Creative Leadership in the early 2000s.
- **Usage:** Used to provide clear, specific, and actionable feedback.
- **Description:** The SBI Model helps in delivering feedback by breaking it down into three components:
  - **Situation:** Describe the specific situation where the behavior occurred.
  - **Behavior:** Detail the observable behavior that occurred.
  - **Impact:** Explain the impact of the behavior on others, the team, or the organization.

The Feedback Sandwich
- **Origin:** Popularized in management training in the 1980s.
- **Usage:** To deliver constructive feedback in a balanced manner.
- **Description:** The Feedback Sandwich technique involves structuring feedback by placing constructive criticism between

positive comments. This approach helps in making the feedback more palatable and maintaining the coachee's motivation.

By incorporating these techniques and models into your coaching practice, you can provide feedback that is not only constructive but also motivational and actionable. Effective feedback fosters a culture of continuous improvement and development, helping your coachees reach their full potential. Remember, the goal is to guide your coachees with clarity, empathy, and a commitment to their growth.

Part 3

Coaching Performance (Goal Setting and Continuous Improvement)

CHAPTER 7

Setting SMART Goals

> "A goal properly set is halfway reached."
> —Zig Ziglar

Setting clear and achievable goals is fundamental to driving performance. SMART goals provide a framework for setting goals that are Specific, Measurable, Achievable, Relevant, and Time-bound. In this chapter, you will learn how to set SMART goals and align them with broader organizational objectives.

The Importance of Setting Clear Goals

Goals are the driving force behind progress and success. They provide direction, focus, and motivation. Without clear goals, it's easy to lose sight of what you're trying to achieve, and performance can suffer as a result. Setting goals that are well-defined and achievable ensures that both the coach and the coachee are aligned and working towards a common purpose.

Introducing SMART Goals

SMART goals are a proven framework for setting objectives that are clear and attainable. The SMART acronym stands for:

- **Specific:** Clearly define the goal.
- **Measurable:** Ensure the goal is quantifiable.
- **Achievable:** Set realistic and attainable goals.
- **Relevant:** Align the goal with broader objectives.
- **Time-bound:** Set a deadline for achieving the goal.

Breaking Down the SMART Framework

Specific

A specific goal clearly states what is to be achieved. It answers the questions: What do I want to accomplish? Why is this goal important? Who is involved? Where is it located? Which resources or limits are involved?

Example:
- Instead of: "Improve sales."
- Use: "Increase sales of Product X by 20% in the North American market."

Measurable

A measurable goal includes criteria to track progress and determine when the goal is met. It answers the question: How will I know when it is accomplished?

Example:
- Instead of: "Improve customer satisfaction."
- Use: "Achieve a 90% customer satisfaction rating on post-support surveys."

Achievable

An achievable goal is realistic and attainable given the available resources and constraints. It answers the question: How can I accomplish this goal? How realistic is the goal based on other constraints?

Example:
- Instead of: "Double sales in one month."
- Use: "Increase sales by 15% over the next quarter."

Relevant

A relevant goal aligns with broader business objectives and is worthwhile. It answers the question: Does this goal matter? Is it the right time? Does it align with our other goals?

Example:
- Instead of: "Launch a new product in an unrelated market."
- Use: "Expand our product line in response to increasing customer demand for eco-friendly options."

Time-bound

A time-bound goal has a clearly defined deadline. It answers the questions: When will this goal be achieved? What can I do six months from now? What can I do six weeks from now? What can I do today?

Example:
- Instead of: "Reduce costs."
- Use: "Reduce operational costs by 10% within the next fiscal year."

Aligning Goals with Organizational Objectives

Setting SMART goals is essential, but it's equally important to ensure that these goals align with broader organizational objectives. This alignment ensures that individual efforts contribute to the overall success of the organization.

Steps to Align Goals

1. **Understand Organizational Objectives:** Familiarize yourself with the company's mission, vision, and strategic goals.
2. **Set Departmental Goals:** Break down organizational objectives into departmental goals.
3. **Translate into Individual Goals:** Ensure each coachee's goals support departmental and organizational goals.

4. **Communicate the Big Picture:** Help coachees see how their work contributes to the organization's success.

Example:
- **Organizational Objective:** Increase market share by 10% in the next year.
- **Departmental Goal:** Launch three new marketing campaigns in Q1 to drive brand awareness.
- **Individual Goal:** Develop and execute a social media campaign to increase brand engagement by 15% in Q1.

Techniques for Setting SMART Goals

Goal Setting Workshops

Conduct workshops to collaboratively set goals with your team. These workshops help ensure buy-in and alignment.

Steps:
1. Present the organizational objectives.
2. Break into smaller groups to brainstorm relevant goals.
3. Refine goals using the SMART framework.
4. Share and discuss goals with the larger group.

Regular Check-ins

Schedule regular check-ins to review progress on goals, provide support, and make adjustments as needed.

Steps:
1. Review the goal and progress to date.
2. Discuss any challenges or obstacles.
3. Adjust the action plan if necessary.
4. Celebrate successes and provide constructive feedback.

Use of Technology

Utilize goal-setting software to track and manage goals. Tools like OKR (Objectives and Key Results) platforms can help maintain visibility and accountability.

Steps:
1. Input goals into the platform.
2. Set reminders and milestones.
3. Monitor progress and update regularly.
4. Generate reports for review meetings.

Scenario: Using SMART Goals for a Sales Representative

Context: David is a sales representative at a mid-sized tech company. He has shown great potential in his role but struggles with consistent performance. During a one-on-one meeting, his manager, Maria, decides to help him set SMART goals to improve his client engagement and sales numbers.

Specific: Maria and David discuss the need for him to increase his client engagement to boost sales. They agree on a clear, specific goal: "Increase the number of client meetings."

Measurable: To track progress, they decide to quantify the goal. They set a measurable target: "Increase client meetings by 20% each month."

Achievable: Considering David's current performance and the average number of client meetings other sales reps conduct, they determine that a 20% increase is challenging but achievable. They discuss strategies and tools he can use, such as better time management, CRM software, and support from the sales team.

Relevant: The goal aligns with the company's broader objective of increasing sales revenue. More client meetings are directly related to potential sales growth. Maria ensures David understands how his increased client engagement contributes to the company's success.

Time-bound: To create a sense of urgency and focus, they set a deadline: "Achieve this goal by the end of the next quarter."

Final SMART Goal: "Increase client meetings by 20% each month, tracked using CRM software, to be achieved by the end of the next quarter."

Detailed Scenario Execution:

Initial Discussion: Maria: "David, I've noticed that while your sales are good, there's potential for improvement. Let's set a goal to increase your client meetings. This should help boost your overall sales numbers."

David: "I agree. I've been thinking about how to get more face time with clients."

Maria: "Great. Let's make this goal specific. How about we aim to increase your client meetings?"

David: "That sounds good. How many more meetings should I target?"

Defining Measurable: Maria: "Let's aim for a 20% increase in client meetings each month. We'll track this using our CRM software."

David: "20% sounds like a good target. I can definitely track it with the CRM."

Ensuring Achievability: Maria: "Considering your current schedule and workload, do you think this increase is achievable?"

David: "It will be a challenge, but I believe it's doable with better time management and using the CRM more efficiently."

Aligning with Relevance: Maria: "Remember, increasing your client meetings is crucial because it directly impacts our overall sales revenue. More meetings should lead to higher sales."

David: "I understand. I can see how this ties into our overall goals."

Setting the Time Frame: Maria: "Let's set a deadline to achieve this by the end of the next quarter. This gives us a clear timeline and allows us to review your progress regularly."

David: "That's a good timeframe. It gives me enough time to adjust and improve."

Finalizing the SMART Goal: Maria: "So, our goal is: 'Increase client meetings by 20% each month, tracked using CRM software, to be achieved by the end of the next quarter.' Does that sound good?"

David: "Yes, that sounds perfect. I'm ready to get started."

Follow-Up and Monitoring:

Monthly Check-Ins: Maria schedules monthly check-ins with David to review his progress. They use the CRM data to track the number of client meetings and discuss any challenges he faces. During these meetings, Maria offers support and additional resources if needed.

End of Quarter Review: At the end of the quarter, Maria and David review the overall progress. David has increased his client meetings by 22%, exceeding the initial goal. They discuss the strategies that worked well and areas for further improvement.

Recognizing Achievement: Maria acknowledges David's hard work and success in reaching the goal. They also discuss setting new SMART goals to continue his development and maintain his momentum.

By setting and achieving SMART goals, David can focus on specific, measurable outcomes that are challenging yet attainable. This structured approach helps him stay motivated and aligned with the company's broader objectives, ultimately leading to improved performance and professional growth.

Call to Action

1. Work with a coachee to set three SMART goals related to their professional development.

Your Notes:

_____
_____
_____
_____
_____
_____
_____
_____

2. Align these goals with broader organizational objectives.

Your Notes:

_____
_____
_____
_____
_____
_____
_____

3. Schedule regular check-ins to monitor progress towards these goals.

Your Notes:

_____

_____

_____

_____

_____

_____

_____

_____

Techniques and Models for Setting SMART Goals

SMART Goals
- **Origin:** First mentioned by George T. Doran in 1981.
- **Usage:** To create clear and achievable goals.
- **Description:** SMART is a mnemonic acronym, giving criteria to guide in the setting of objectives. It stands for Specific, Measurable, Achievable, Relevant, and Time-bound. Each element of the SMART framework works together to create a goal that is carefully planned and trackable.

OKRs (Objectives and Key Results)
- **Origin:** Developed by Andy Grove at Intel in the 1970s.
- **Usage:** To set and communicate company, team, and personal goals and their measurable outcomes.
- **Description:** OKRs stand for Objectives and Key Results. Objectives define what you want to achieve, and Key Results are the specific, measurable outcomes that will achieve the Objective.

By using these techniques and models, you can ensure that your coachees set goals that are not only SMART but also aligned with the larger objectives of the organization. This alignment drives focused effort and meaningful progress, contributing to both individual and organizational success. Remember, the key to effective goal setting is clarity, alignment, and continuous review. Let's work together to set the stage for success, one SMART goal at a time.

CHAPTER 8

Creating a Culture of Continuous Improvement

"Continuous improvement is better than delayed perfection."
—Mark Twain

Aculture of continuous improvement fosters ongoing development and excellence. In this chapter, we will explore how to implement continuous improvement initiatives using Lean Six Sigma principles, specifically focusing on Kaizen and the PDCA cycle. Creating this culture encourages your coachee to constantly seek ways to improve and innovate, leading to sustained growth and success.

The Importance of Continuous Improvement

Continuous improvement is not just a buzzword; it's a mindset that drives organizations towards excellence. It involves making incremental changes regularly to improve processes, products, and services. This approach not only enhances efficiency and effectiveness but also empowers individuals to contribute to the organization's success.

The Lean Six Sigma Approach

Lean Six Sigma is a methodology that combines Lean's focus on reducing waste with Six Sigma's emphasis on reducing variation. This powerful combination provides a structured approach to problem-solving and process improvement.

Introducing Kaizen

What is Kaizen?

Kaizen is a Japanese term meaning "change for better" or "continuous improvement." It involves everyone in the organization, from top management to front-line employees, working together to make small, incremental changes regularly. The philosophy behind Kaizen is that even small changes can have a significant impact over time.

Implementing Kaizen

1. **Identify Opportunities for Improvement:**
   - Encourage coachees to observe their work processes and identify areas where improvements can be made.
   - Use tools like Value Stream Mapping to visualize and analyze the flow of materials and information.
2. **Engage Everyone:**
   - Foster a culture where everyone feels responsible for improvement.
   - Conduct regular Kaizen events or workshops to brainstorm and implement improvements.
3. **Standardize Improvements:**
   - Document the improved processes and standardize them to ensure they are consistently followed.
   - Use Standard Operating Procedures (SOPs) to maintain the improvements.

Scenario: Implementing Kaizen for Process Improvement

Context: Sam is a team leader at a financial services company. She has observed that her team spends a considerable amount of time on manual data entry tasks, which is not only time-consuming but also prone to errors. Recognizing the need for improvement, Sam decides to organize a Kaizen event to identify and implement a more efficient solution.

Initial Observation: Sam: "I've noticed that we are spending a lot of our time on manual data entry. This is affecting our productivity and increasing the chance of errors. I think we can find a better way to handle this."

Kaizen Event Preparation: Sam prepares for the Kaizen event by gathering data on the current process and its impact on the team's workload and accuracy. She invites team members to participate, ensuring they understand the goal is to improve the process and make their work easier.

Kaizen Event:
Brainstorming Solutions: Sam: "Let's brainstorm ideas to reduce the time we spend on manual data entry and improve accuracy. No idea is too big or too small."

Team Member 1: "We could look into software that automates data entry. I've heard there are tools that can integrate with our current systems."

Team Member 2: "What about using templates that can auto-populate some of the fields based on previous entries?"

Team Member 3: "We could also have a checklist to ensure all data is entered correctly, which might help reduce errors."

Evaluating Options: Sam: "These are great ideas. Let's evaluate them based on feasibility, cost, and potential impact. Automating data entry seems like it could save us the most time and significantly reduce errors."

Decision and Action Plan: After evaluating the options, the team decides to implement a new software tool that automates data entry.

Sam: "We've decided to go with the software automation. Here's the plan:
1. Research and select the best software tool for our needs.
2. Set up a trial run with a small segment of our data.
3. Train the team on how to use the new tool.
4. Monitor the results and make adjustments as necessary."

Implementation:
Research and Selection: The team researches various software options and selects one that integrates well with their existing systems and has a user-friendly interface.

Trial Run: Sam: "We'll start with a trial run next week. I need a few volunteers to test the new tool with a portion of our data."

Team Member 1: "I'll volunteer. I'm excited to see how this works."

Training: Sam organizes a training session for the team to ensure everyone is comfortable using the new software.

Monitoring and Adjustments: Over the next few weeks, the team uses the new tool and provides feedback. Sam monitors the process closely and makes minor adjustments to improve the tool's efficiency and address any issues.

Outcome:
Improved Efficiency: Sam: "Since implementing the new software, we've saved a significant amount of time on data entry. Our error rate has also decreased dramatically."

Team Member 2: "I've noticed I have more time to focus on other important tasks. This tool has really made a difference."

Team Feedback: Sam: "I want to thank everyone for their participation and input during the Kaizen event. Your contributions have been invaluable, and we've achieved great results together."

Reflecting on the Kaizen Process: Sam: "This experience has shown us the power of continuous improvement. By working together and focusing on small, incremental changes, we can significantly improve our processes and overall efficiency."

Final Reflection: Sam and her team celebrate their success and discuss other areas where they can apply the Kaizen approach. They recognize the importance of regularly reviewing their processes and seeking opportunities for improvement.

By organizing a Kaizen event and involving her team in the process, Sam not only improved the efficiency and accuracy of their data entry tasks but also fostered a culture of continuous improvement. This scenario highlights the benefits of collaborative problem-solving and the impact of small, incremental changes on overall productivity and team morale.

The PDCA Cycle

What is the PDCA Cycle?

The PDCA (Plan-Do-Check-Act) cycle, also known as the Deming cycle, is a four-step model for carrying out change. It provides a structured approach to problem-solving and continuous improvement.

Implementing the PDCA Cycle

1. **Plan:**
   - ○ Identify the problem or opportunity for improvement.
   - ○ Develop a plan to address the problem, including specific objectives and actions.
   - ○ Use tools like Fishbone Diagrams and 5 Whys to identify root causes.

2. **Do:**
   - ○ Implement the plan on a small scale to test its effectiveness.
   - ○ Ensure that all stakeholders are aware of and involved in the implementation.

3. **Check:**
   - ○ Monitor and measure the results of the implementation.
   - ○ Compare the results against the objectives to determine if the plan was successful.

4. **Act:**
   - If the plan was successful, implement it on a larger scale and standardize the process.
   - If the plan was not successful, refine and adjust the plan based on the lessons learned and repeat the cycle.

Scenario: Implementing the PDCA Cycle to Improve Customer Satisfaction

Context: Jm is a sales manager at a software company. He has noticed a high rate of customer dissatisfaction based on recent feedback and survey results. Determined to address this issue, Jim decides to use the PDCA (Plan-Do-Check-Act) cycle to identify and solve the problem.

Initial Observation: Jim: "I've been reviewing our customer feedback, and it's clear we have an issue with customer satisfaction. We need to find the root cause and fix it to maintain our client relationships and improve retention."

PDCA Cycle Implementation:
Plan: Identify the Root Cause Jim begins by gathering data on customer feedback and analyzing patterns. He involves his sales team to get their insights and observations.

Jim: "Let's start by collecting data on the feedback. We'll look at the type of complaints, frequency, and when they occur. I also want to hear from you about any recurring issues or trends you've noticed in your interactions with customers."

Team Member 1: "I've noticed that a lot of complaints come after the initial onboarding phase. Customers seem to feel unsupported once the software is implemented."

Team Member 2: "It seems like our follow-up processes vary a lot between different sales reps, which might be causing inconsistencies."

John: "Good observations. It sounds like our follow-up and support processes might be the issue. We'll focus on standardizing these processes."

Do: Test the Solution Jim decides to test a new standardized follow-up process with a small group of new customers to see if it improves satisfaction.

Jim: "We'll start by testing a standardized follow-up process with the next five customers we onboard. I need everyone to follow the new process strictly and document any changes or feedback."

Team Member 1: "I'll keep a close eye on the customer interactions and make sure they remain consistent."

Check: Monitor and Analyze Results After a month, Jim and his team review the feedback to see if the new follow-up process has made a difference.

Jim: "The initial results are promising. We've seen a 40% increase in positive feedback from the customers who experienced the new follow-up process. Let's compare this with the feedback from other customers to confirm the impact."

Team Member 2: "The other customers still have higher dissatisfaction rates, confirming that the standardized follow-up process is working well."

Act: Implement the Solution Across All Customer Accounts Jim decides to implement the standardized follow-up process across all customer accounts based on the successful trial.

Jim: "Given the positive results from our trial, we'll now roll out the standardized follow-up process to all our customer accounts. I'll also provide training to ensure everyone understands the new protocol."

Team Member 1: "I'll help with the training and make sure everyone is on the same page."

Outcome:
Sustained Improvement in Customer Satisfaction Jim: "Since standardizing the follow-up process, we've seen a significant and sustained improvement in customer satisfaction. This improvement not only enhances customer relationships but also increases retention rates."

Team Member 2: "The process feels more consistent now, and we're able to maintain customer satisfaction more easily."

Reflecting on the PDCA Process: Jim: "This experience with the PDCA cycle has shown us the importance of methodical problem-solving. By planning carefully, testing solutions, checking results, and then acting on those results, we can achieve substantial improvements."

Final Reflection: Jim and his team celebrate their success and discuss other areas where the PDCA cycle can be applied. They recognize the value of continuous improvement and commit to regularly reviewing and optimizing their processes.

By implementing the PDCA cycle and involving his team in the process, Jim successfully improved customer satisfaction, enhancing overall client relationships and retention rates. This scenario highlights the effectiveness of the PDCA cycle in systematic problem-solving and continuous improvement within a sales or customer-facing organization.

Creating a Culture of Continuous Improvement

Steps to Foster a Continuous Improvement Culture
1. **Leadership Commitment:**
   - Leaders must demonstrate a commitment to continuous improvement by setting the example and providing necessary resources.
   - Communicate the importance of continuous improvement and recognize contributions.
2. **Employee Empowerment:**
   - Empower employees to take ownership of improvement initiatives.
   - Provide training on Lean Six Sigma principles and tools.
3. **Regular Review and Feedback:**
   - Conduct regular review meetings to discuss progress and identify new improvement opportunities.
   - Provide constructive feedback and celebrate successes.
4. **Open Communication:**
   - Foster an environment where open communication is encouraged.
   - Use suggestion boxes, regular meetings, and digital platforms to gather ideas.
5. **Continuous Learning:**
   - Encourage a mindset of continuous learning and development.
   - Provide opportunities for professional development and cross-training.

Scenario: Implementing a Continuous Improvement Program to Enhance Employee Engagement

Context: Maria is an HR manager at a mid-sized tech company. She has noticed a decline in employee engagement and a lack of enthusiasm for company initiatives. Determined to address this, Maria decides to implement a continuous improvement program that encourages employees to contribute their ideas for enhancing the workplace.

Initial Observation: Maria: "Our recent employee engagement survey shows that many of our team members feel disconnected and uninspired. We need a strategy to boost engagement and make everyone feel more invested in our company's success."

Continuous Improvement Program Implementation:
Step 1: Introduce the Program Maria launches the continuous improvement program during an all-hands meeting, explaining its purpose and how it will work.

Maria: "I'm excited to introduce our new continuous improvement program. This initiative is designed to give everyone a voice in how we can improve our processes and workplace. You can submit any ideas you have for making our company better. Every quarter, we'll review the submissions and implement the best ones."

Step 2: Encourage Participation To ensure everyone feels encouraged to participate, Maria provides multiple channels for idea submission, including an online portal, suggestion boxes, and regular brainstorming sessions.

Maria: "You can submit your ideas through our new online portal, drop them in the suggestion boxes placed around the office, or bring them up during our weekly brainstorming sessions. We want to hear from everyone!"

Employee 1: "I have some ideas on how we can streamline our onboarding process. I'll submit them through the portal."

Employee 2: "I think we could improve our team collaboration with some new tools. I'll bring it up in the next brainstorming session."

Step 3: Review and Implement Ideas Each quarter, Maria and a committee of representatives from different departments review the submitted ideas and select the most promising ones for implementation.

Maria: "Thank you all for your fantastic ideas. We've selected five that we believe will make a significant impact. We'll start implementing these changes next month, and I'm excited to see the results."

Employee 1: "I'm thrilled that my idea about improving the onboarding process was chosen. I can't wait to see it in action."

Employee 2: "It's great to see my suggestion for new collaboration tools being taken seriously."

Step 4: Recognize and Reward Contributions To further motivate employees, Maria introduces a recognition and reward system for those whose ideas are implemented. Each quarter, the contributors of the best ideas are celebrated and receive a reward.

Maria: "I want to recognize and thank everyone whose ideas were implemented this quarter. Your contributions are invaluable, and as a token of our appreciation, we have a small reward for each of you."

Employee 1: "It's encouraging to see our ideas being valued and rewarded. It makes me feel more connected to the company."

Employee 2: "The recognition and reward system is a great motivator. I'm already thinking about what to suggest next."

Outcome:

Increased Engagement and Ownership Maria: "Since launching the continuous improvement program, we've seen a significant increase in employee engagement. People feel more involved and invested in our success, and it's wonderful to see so many innovative ideas coming to life."

Employee 1: "The new onboarding process is much smoother now, and new hires are getting up to speed faster."

Employee 2: "The new collaboration tools have really improved our teamwork and communication."

Reflecting on the Continuous Improvement Program: Maria: "This program has shown us the power of giving employees a voice and recognizing their contributions. By fostering a culture of continuous improvement, we've not only increased engagement but also driven numerous process improvements that benefit the entire company."

Final Reflection: Maria and her team celebrate the success of the program and discuss ways to further enhance it. They commit to regularly reviewing and optimizing the initiative to ensure it continues to deliver value and maintain high levels of employee engagement.

By implementing a continuous improvement program and actively involving her team, Maria successfully enhanced employee engagement and drove numerous process improvements. This scenario demonstrates the effectiveness of continuous improvement initiatives in fostering a sense of ownership, motivation, and innovation within an organization.

Call to Action

1. Implement a continuous improvement initiative (e.g., a weekly learning session) with your team.

Your Notes:

_____

_____

_____

_____

_____

_____

_____

2. Identify a current process that could benefit from improvement and apply the Kaizen approach.

Your Notes:

_____

_____

_____

_____

_____

_____

_____

3. Use the PDCA cycle to address a specific problem or opportunity for improvement in your organization.

Your Notes:

_____

_____

_____

_____

_____

_____

_____

4. Foster an environment of continuous improvement by encouraging open communication and recognizing contributions.

Your Notes:

_____

_____

_____

_____

_____

_____

Techniques and Models for Continuous Improvement

Kaizen

- **Origin:** Developed in Japan, post-World War II, popularized by Masaaki Imai.
- **Usage:** To foster continuous improvement in processes and systems.
- **Description:** Kaizen involves everyone in the organization working together to make small, incremental changes regularly.

It emphasizes the importance of standardizing improvements and maintaining a culture of continuous improvement.

PDCA Cycle (Plan-Do-Check-Act)

- **Origin:** Developed by Dr. William Edwards Deming in the 1950s.
- **Usage:** To implement continuous improvement processes.
- **Description:** The PDCA Cycle is a four-step model for carrying out change. It stands for Plan (identify a goal and plan the change), Do (implement the change), Check (observe the results and learn from them), and Act (adjust based on what was learned).

By using these Lean Six Sigma principles and tools, you can create a culture of continuous improvement that drives ongoing development and excellence. Encourage your coachees to constantly seek ways to improve and innovate, leading to sustained growth and success. Remember, continuous improvement is a journey, not a destination. Let's embrace this journey together and create a culture of excellence.

CHAPTER 9

Overcoming Obstacles and Staying Motivated

"The difference between a stumbling block and a stepping stone is how high you raise your foot."

—Benny Lewis

C hallenges and setbacks are inevitable, but how you address them can make all the difference. As coaches and leaders, our role is to guide our coachees through these difficult moments, helping them to navigate obstacles and maintain their motivation. In this chapter, we will explore strategies for overcoming challenges and sustaining motivation using techniques like resilience training and fostering intrinsic motivation.

Embracing Challenges as Opportunities

First and foremost, it's essential to shift our mindset towards challenges. Instead of viewing them as roadblocks, we should see them as opportunities for growth and learning. This perspective is crucial for both coaches and coachees. By embracing challenges, we can foster a culture of resilience and continuous improvement.

The Importance of Resilience

Resilience is the ability to bounce back from adversity, to adapt and thrive despite setbacks. It is a critical skill for anyone looking to achieve long-term success. Resilient individuals are not immune to stress or failure, but they have developed the tools and mindset to cope with and overcome these difficulties.

Building Resilience

1. **Develop a Positive Mindset:**
   - Encourage coachees to focus on what they can control and to adopt a positive outlook.
   - Practice gratitude and positive affirmations to reinforce this mindset.

2. **Strengthen Relationships:**
   - Building a support network is crucial. Encourage coachees to cultivate strong relationships with family, friends, and colleagues.
   - Foster a sense of community and belonging within your team.

3. **Enhance Problem-Solving Skills:**
   - Equip coachees with problem-solving techniques such as brainstorming, root cause analysis, and creative thinking.
   - Encourage them to approach problems systematically and to view them as puzzles to be solved.

4. **Encourage Flexibility:**
   - Teach coachees the importance of adaptability and being open to change.
   - Encourage them to see setbacks as opportunities to learn and pivot rather than insurmountable obstacles.

Scenario: Overcoming a Major Project Setback with Resilience and Learning

Context: Daniel is a project manager at a fast-growing tech company. He is responsible for delivering a key project that has significant implications for the company's growth. However, unforeseen technical issues cause major delays, threatening the project's timeline and putting immense pressure on Daniel and his team.

Initial Challenge: Daniel: "We've hit a significant roadblock with our project. The technical issues we're facing have set us back by weeks, and we're at risk of missing our deadlines. This situation is incredibly stressful for everyone involved."

Step 1: Focusing on Controllable Elements Instead of succumbing to the pressure, Daniel decides to focus on the elements he can control. He gathers his team for an emergency meeting to discuss the current situation and brainstorm potential solutions.

Daniel: "I understand the frustration and stress this delay is causing. Let's focus on what we can control. We need to identify the root causes of these technical issues and figure out how to address them effectively."

Team Member 1: "We've identified that the main issue is with the integration of the new software components. It's more complex than we initially anticipated."

Team Member 2: "We also need to improve our communication with the vendor to get quicker responses and support."

Step 2: Leveraging Support Network Daniel reaches out to his support network within the company, including senior leaders and technical experts, to seek advice and additional resources. He ensures his team knows they have the company's backing.

Daniel: "I've spoken with our senior leaders, and they are fully aware of the situation. They've allocated additional resources and connected us with some technical experts who can help us navigate these challenges."

Team Member 1: "That's a relief to hear. Having extra hands and expertise will make a big difference."

Team Member 2: "I'll coordinate with the vendor support team to expedite our communication and troubleshooting process."

Step 3: Reframing the Situation as a Learning Opportunity Daniel encourages his team to view this setback not just as a crisis but as a valuable learning experience. He emphasizes the importance of understanding the root causes and implementing changes to prevent similar issues in the future.

Daniel: "While this situation is far from ideal, it's an opportunity for us to learn and improve. Let's conduct a thorough root cause analysis to understand what went wrong and how we can prevent it from happening again."

Team Member 1: "We'll start documenting the issues and our troubleshooting steps. This will help us create a detailed post-mortem report."

Team Member 2: "We can also update our project management processes to include better risk assessment and mitigation strategies."

Step 4: Implementing Changes and Improvements Based on the insights gained from the root cause analysis, Daniel and his team implement several changes to their processes. They enhance their project planning, improve communication channels, and establish more rigorous testing protocols.

Daniel: "We've identified several key areas for improvement. By updating our project management processes, improving our communication with vendors, and establishing more rigorous testing protocols, we can prevent similar issues in the future."

Team Member 1: "These changes will definitely strengthen our approach and help us manage risks more effectively."

Team Member 2: "I'm confident that with these improvements, we'll be better prepared to handle any future challenges."

Outcome: Immediate Challenge Overcome: Daniel and his team successfully address the technical issues, getting the project back on track and meeting the revised deadlines.

Daniel: "I'm incredibly proud of how our team has handled this setback. We've overcome a major challenge and delivered the project on time, thanks to everyone's hard work and dedication."

Team Member 1: "It was a tough situation, but we pulled through by staying focused and working together."

Team Member 2: "I've learned a lot from this experience, and I'm confident we're now better equipped to handle future challenges."

Strengthened Team Resilience: Daniel's leadership and the team's collaborative efforts have strengthened their resilience, making them more prepared for future setbacks.

Daniel: "This experience has shown us the importance of resilience and continuous improvement. We're now a stronger, more cohesive team, ready to tackle whatever challenges come our way."

Team Member 1: "I feel more confident in our ability to handle future setbacks, knowing that we have the right processes and support in place."

Team Member 2: "This experience has brought us closer as a team and has reinforced the importance of learning and adapting."

Final Reflection: Daniel reflects on the situation and the lessons learned, emphasizing the importance of focusing on controllable elements, leveraging support networks, and viewing challenges as learning opportunities.

Daniel: "This project taught me the value of focusing on what we can control, seeking support when needed, and turning setbacks into learning opportunities. These principles have not only helped us overcome this challenge but have also prepared us for future success."

By focusing on controllable elements, leveraging his support network, and reframing the setback as a learning opportunity, Daniel successfully overcame a major project delay. This scenario demonstrates the power of resilience and continuous improvement in handling challenges and strengthening team performance.

BONUS CONTENT

Root Cause Analysis: Uncovering the Underlying Issues

Root Cause Analysis (RCA) is a systematic process used to identify the fundamental reasons behind a problem or issue. By focusing on the root cause rather than the symptoms, organizations can implement effective solutions that prevent recurrence. This approach is essential in creating a culture of continuous improvement and ensuring long-term success.

Importance of Root Cause Analysis
1. Prevent Recurrence: Identifying and addressing the root cause ensures that the problem does not happen again.
2. Improve Processes: Understanding the underlying issues helps in refining processes and systems.
3. Increase Efficiency: By solving the root cause, resources are used more effectively, reducing wasted effort on temporary fixes.
4. Enhance Quality: Root cause analysis contributes to higher quality outputs by eliminating the sources of defects or problems.
5. Foster Learning: Encourages a culture of learning and improvement within the organization.

Steps in Root Cause Analysis

1. Define the Problem: Clearly articulate the issue at hand, ensuring all stakeholders have a common understanding.

2. Collect Data: Gather relevant data and information related to the problem. This includes historical data, process logs, and feedback from involved parties.

3. Identify Possible Causes: Use brainstorming sessions or tools like Fishbone Diagrams (Ishikawa) and 5 Whys to explore potential causes.

4. Determine Root Cause: Analyze the identified causes to pinpoint the fundamental reason for the problem. This may involve testing hypotheses and validating findings.

5. Implement Solutions: Develop and implement corrective actions aimed at addressing the root cause. Ensure these solutions are practical and sustainable.

6. Monitor and Review: Track the effectiveness of the implemented solutions. Make adjustments as necessary and ensure the problem does not recur.

Common Techniques for Root Cause Analysis

1. 5 Whys:
    - Origin: Developed by Sakichi Toyoda and used within the Toyota Production System.
    - Usage: Asking "why" repeatedly (typically five times) to drill down into the root cause of a problem.
    - Example:
        - Problem: The car won't start.
        - Why 1: The battery is dead.
        - Why 2: The alternator is not functioning.
        - Why 3: The alternator belt is broken.
        - Why 4: The belt was well beyond its useful life and not replaced.

- Why 5: The vehicle was not maintained according to the recommended service schedule.
- Root Cause: Lack of regular vehicle maintenance.

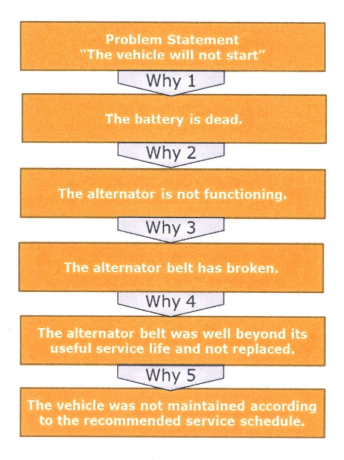

2. Fishbone Diagram (Ishikawa):
   ○ Origin: Developed by Kaoru Ishikawa in the 1960s.
   ○ Usage: Visual tool to identify, explore, and display potential causes of a specific problem. The diagram resembles a fish skeleton with the problem at the head and potential causes as bones.
   ○ Categories: Common categories include People, Processes, Materials, Equipment, Environment, and Management.

- Example:
  - Problem: Product defect.
  - Categories and potential causes:
    - People: Inadequate training, lack of skills.
    - Processes: Inefficient procedures, lack of quality control.
    - Materials: Poor quality raw materials, inconsistent supply.
    - Equipment: Malfunctioning machinery, outdated technology.
    - Environment: Poor lighting, high humidity.
    - Management: Lack of supervision, unclear instructions.

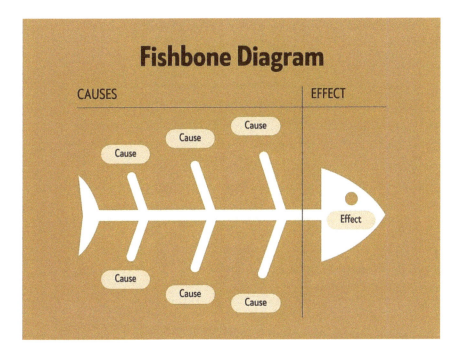

3. Pareto Analysis:
   - Origin: Based on the Pareto Principle (80/20 rule) by Vilfredo Pareto.

- Usage: Identifying the most significant factors contributing to a problem by focusing on the "vital few" causes that have the most impact.
- Example:
  - Problem: High customer complaints.
  - Data analysis shows 80% of complaints come from 20% of causes, such as poor customer service and delayed delivery.
  - Focus: Addressing these key issues will significantly reduce overall complaints.
4. Failure Mode and Effects Analysis (FMEA):
   - Origin: Developed in the 1940s by the U.S. military and later adopted by various industries.
   - Usage: Systematic method for evaluating processes to identify where and how they might fail and assessing the relative impact of different failures.
   - Steps:
     - Identify failure modes.
     - Determine the effects of each failure mode.
     - Assess the severity, occurrence, and detection of each failure mode.
     - Prioritize failure modes based on risk and develop mitigation plans.
   - Example:
     - Process: Manufacturing of a component.
     - Failure Modes: Material defects, incorrect assembly, inadequate testing.
     - Effects: Product failure, customer dissatisfaction, increased costs.
     - Mitigation: Implementing rigorous material inspections, automated assembly checks, and comprehensive testing protocols.

Implementing Root Cause Analysis in Your Organization

1. Training and Awareness: Ensure all employees understand the importance of RCA and are trained in relevant techniques.
2. Collaboration: Foster a culture of collaboration where team members can openly discuss issues and potential solutions.
3. Documentation: Keep detailed records of RCA processes, findings, and implemented solutions to track progress and share learnings.
4. Continuous Improvement: Regularly review and refine RCA processes to adapt to new challenges and improve effectiveness.

Techniques for Building Resilience

Cognitive Behavioral Strategies

Cognitive Behavioral Therapy (CBT) techniques can be highly effective in building resilience. These strategies help individuals to identify and change negative thought patterns, enabling them to respond to challenges more constructively.

1. **Thought Records:**
   - Encourage coachees to keep a journal of their thoughts and feelings, especially during stressful situations.
   - This practice helps them to identify negative thought patterns and replace them with more positive and constructive ones.
2. **Reframing:**
   - Teach coachees to reframe negative situations by looking for any positive aspects or potential learning opportunities.
   - This technique helps to shift their focus from what's going wrong to what can be learned or gained from the experience.

Scenario: Sarah, a Sales Executive, Overcomes Negative Thoughts with Reframing

Context: Sarah is a high-performing sales executive at a leading technology company. Despite her success, she often finds herself overwhelmed by negative thoughts when deals don't go as planned. These setbacks affect her confidence and overall well-being, creating a cycle of stress and self-doubt.

Initial Challenge: Sarah: "I've been struggling with negative thoughts every time a deal falls through. It's affecting my performance and making it hard to stay motivated. I need to find a way to break this cycle."

Step 1: Keeping a Thought Record To address this issue, Sarah decides to start keeping a thought record. She documents her thoughts and feelings whenever a deal doesn't go as planned, noting down specific triggers and her emotional responses.

Sarah: "I'm going to start writing down my thoughts and feelings every time I lose a deal. By identifying the patterns, I hope to understand what's triggering my negative thoughts."

Example Thought Record:
- Trigger: Lost a major client deal
- Thought: "I'm not good enough at my job."
- Feeling: Overwhelmed, anxious, and demotivated

Step 2: Analyzing and Identifying Patterns After a few weeks of maintaining her thought record, Sarah notices recurring patterns in her negative thoughts. She realizes that her self-doubt often stems from unrealistic expectations and a fear of failure.

Sarah: "I've noticed that my negative thoughts are usually triggered by a fear of failure and unrealistic expectations. I need to find a way to challenge and reframe these thoughts."

Step 3: Practicing Reframing Techniques Sarah decides to practice reframing her negative thoughts. She uses cognitive behavioral techniques to challenge her initial reactions and replace them with more constructive perspectives.

Sarah: "Instead of focusing on my fear of failure, I'm going to reframe these setbacks as opportunities to learn and improve my sales techniques."

Example Reframed Thought:
- Original Thought: "I'm not good enough at my job."
- Reframed Thought: "This setback is an opportunity to refine my sales approach and learn from my experiences."

Step 4: Implementing Changes and Building Resilience Sarah begins to see her setbacks as learning opportunities. She reviews her sales techniques and seeks feedback from colleagues and mentors to identify areas for improvement. This proactive approach helps her build resilience and maintain a positive outlook.

Sarah: "By viewing setbacks as learning opportunities, I'm more motivated to improve my skills. I'm also seeking feedback from my colleagues and mentors to ensure I'm continuously growing."

Outcome: Enhanced Performance and Well-Being: Sarah's shift in perspective significantly enhances her performance and overall well-being. She becomes more resilient, confident, and better equipped to handle setbacks.

Sarah: "I've noticed a significant improvement in my performance and well-being. By reframing my negative thoughts, I'm able to stay focused and motivated, even when things don't go as planned."

Colleague: "Sarah, I've seen a noticeable change in your attitude and performance. Your ability to bounce back from setbacks is truly inspiring."

Final Reflection: Sarah reflects on her journey and the impact of reframing on her performance and well-being. She encourages others to adopt similar techniques to overcome negative thoughts and build resilience.

Sarah: "This experience has taught me the power of reframing and the importance of viewing setbacks as opportunities for growth. I encourage everyone to practice these techniques to build resilience and improve their performance."

By keeping a thought record and practicing reframing, Sarah learns to view setbacks as opportunities to refine her sales techniques and improve her resilience. This shift in perspective significantly enhances her performance and overall well-being, demonstrating the power of cognitive behavioral techniques in overcoming negative thoughts and building resilience.

Intrinsic Motivation: The Key to Sustained Drive

Intrinsic motivation comes from within. It is the drive to do something because it is inherently interesting or enjoyable, not because of external rewards or pressures. Your people are more likely to take action (and find that action reward) when the action is intrinsically motivated. Fostering intrinsic motivation is crucial for maintaining long-term engagement and commitment.

Fostering Intrinsic Motivation

1. **Autonomy:**
   - Give coachees control over their work and decision-making processes.
   - Allow them to choose how they approach tasks and projects, providing a sense of ownership and responsibility.
2. **Mastery:**
   - Encourage coachees to pursue mastery in their skills and competencies.
   - Provide opportunities for continuous learning and development, such as training programs, workshops, and stretch assignments.
3. **Purpose:**
   - Help coachees connect their work to a larger purpose or mission.
   - Highlight how their contributions impact the team, organization, and broader community.

Scenario: James, a Software Developer, Revitalizes Motivation Through Autonomy and Purpose

Context: James is a talented software developer at a fast-paced tech company. Despite his skills, he's been feeling demotivated and uninspired by the routine tasks he handles daily. His manager, recognizing James's potential, decides to take action to help him regain his enthusiasm and drive.

Initial Challenge: James: "I've been feeling really stuck and unmotivated lately. The routine tasks are draining my energy, and I'm not finding my work fulfilling anymore."

Manager: "I've noticed that you seem less engaged lately. Let's find a way to reignite your passion for your work. I think taking on a new project that challenges you and aligns with your interests might help."

Step 1: Identifying Interests and Goals To address the issue, James's manager sits down with him to discuss his interests and professional goals. They identify areas where James wants to grow and the types of projects that excite him.

James: "I'm really interested in machine learning and would love to work on a project that allows me to develop my skills in that area."

Manager: "Great! Let's find a project that aligns with your interests and provides the challenge you're looking for."

Step 2: Assigning a New, Challenging Project The manager assigns James a new project focused on developing a machine learning algorithm for a key company initiative. This project aligns with James's interests and offers a significant challenge, pushing him out of his routine and into a space where he can grow and innovate.

Manager: "I'm assigning you to lead the development of our new machine learning algorithm. This project will be challenging but I believe it's a perfect match for your skills and interests."

Step 3: Providing Autonomy and Clear Purpose To enhance James's intrinsic motivation, his manager ensures he has the autonomy to make key decisions and shape the project. Additionally, the project's goals are clearly tied to the company's larger mission, giving James a strong sense of purpose.

Manager: "You'll have full autonomy to make decisions on this project. We're counting on your expertise to guide us. This algorithm will play a crucial role in our new product line, directly impacting our company's success."

Step 4: Creating Opportunities for Mastery The manager supports James's growth by providing opportunities for him to learn and master new skills. This includes access to relevant training, resources, and mentorship from senior developers.

Manager: "I've arranged for you to attend a workshop on advanced machine learning techniques. Additionally, you can reach out to our senior developers for guidance and mentorship whenever needed."

Outcome: Increased Intrinsic Motivation and Job Satisfaction: With autonomy, opportunities for mastery, and a clear sense of purpose, James's intrinsic motivation soars. He becomes highly engaged in his work, leading to increased productivity and job satisfaction.

James: "Taking on this project has reignited my passion for my work. I feel challenged and motivated, and I'm learning so much. It's great to see how my efforts are directly contributing to the company's success."

Manager: "Your enthusiasm and productivity have been incredible, James. The impact of your work is already noticeable, and I'm excited to see what you'll achieve next."

Final Reflection: James reflects on his journey and the impact of taking on a challenging project that aligns with his interests. He encourages others to seek out opportunities that provide autonomy, mastery, and a sense of purpose to enhance their motivation and job satisfaction.

James: "This experience has shown me the importance of aligning work with my interests and having the autonomy to make meaningful decisions. I encourage everyone to seek out opportunities that challenge and excite them—it makes a world of difference."

By giving James autonomy, opportunities for mastery, and a clear sense of purpose, his intrinsic motivation soared, leading to higher productivity and job satisfaction. This scenario highlights the power of leveraging intrinsic motivation to enhance engagement and performance in the workplace.

Techniques for Fostering Intrinsic Motivation

Self-Determination Theory (SDT)
Self-Determination Theory, developed by psychologists Edward Deci and Richard Ryan, posits that people are most motivated when they feel autonomous, competent, and connected to others. Applying SDT principles can significantly enhance intrinsic motivation.

1. **Autonomy-Supportive Environment:**
   - Create a work environment that supports autonomy by involving coachees in decision-making and respecting their input.
   - Avoid micromanagement and instead provide guidance and support as needed.
2. **Competence Building:**
   - Provide regular feedback that focuses on strengths and areas for improvement.
   - Offer challenges that are appropriately matched to the coachee's skill level to promote growth without causing undue stress.
3. **Relatedness:**
   - Foster a sense of community and connection within the team.
   - Encourage collaborative projects and team-building activities to strengthen relationships.

Scenario: Emily, a Healthcare Administrator, Reignites Motivation Through Autonomy, Mastery, and Support

Context: Emily is a dedicated healthcare administrator who has been feeling overwhelmed and burnt out by the constant demands and high pressure of her role. Recognizing the signs of burnout, her supervisor decides to apply the principles of Self-Determination Theory (SDT) to help Emily regain her motivation and job satisfaction.

Initial Challenge: Emily: "I've been feeling exhausted and burnt out lately. The workload is intense, and I'm struggling to stay motivated."

Supervisor: "I understand how challenging your role can be. Let's work together to find a way to alleviate some of that stress and help you feel more engaged and motivated in your work."

Step 1: Providing Autonomy To address the issue of burnout, Emily's supervisor begins by giving her more control over her projects and responsibilities. This involves allowing Emily to choose the projects she is most passionate about and giving her the freedom to make decisions on how to approach them.

Supervisor: "I'd like to give you more autonomy over your projects. You can select the ones you're most interested in and decide how you want to manage them. This should help you feel more in control and engaged."

Emily: "I appreciate that. Having the ability to choose my projects and how to approach them will definitely help me feel more invested in my work."

Step 2: Enhancing Skills and Mastery Next, the supervisor focuses on providing targeted feedback and opportunities for Emily to develop her skills. This includes offering training programs, workshops, and one-on-

one mentoring to help Emily enhance her competencies and feel more confident in her abilities.

Supervisor: "I've arranged for you to attend a workshop on advanced healthcare management techniques. Additionally, I'm available for one-on-one mentoring sessions to help you navigate any challenges you face."

Emily: "Thank you for the opportunity. Improving my skills will help me feel more capable and reduce some of the stress I've been experiencing."

Step 3: Fostering a Supportive Team Environment The supervisor also works on fostering a supportive team environment by encouraging open communication, collaboration, and mutual support among team members. This includes regular team meetings, social events, and peer recognition programs to create a sense of community and belonging.

Supervisor: "We're going to have regular team meetings where everyone can share their experiences and support each other. I also want to introduce a peer recognition program to celebrate our successes together."

Emily: "Having a supportive team environment will make a big difference. It's reassuring to know that we can rely on each other and celebrate our achievements together."

Outcome: Reignited Intrinsic Motivation and Improved Performance: With more autonomy, opportunities for mastery, and a supportive team environment, Emily's intrinsic motivation is reignited. She feels more in control, competent, and connected to her work, leading to improved performance and job satisfaction.

Emily: "Having control over my projects and the chance to develop my skills has made a huge difference. I feel more motivated and less stressed. The supportive team environment also helps me stay positive and focused."

Supervisor: "I've noticed a significant improvement in your performance and overall well-being, Emily. Your renewed motivation is inspiring, and it's great to see you thriving again."

Final Reflection: Emily reflects on her journey from burnout to renewed motivation and encourages others to seek out environments that provide autonomy, opportunities for mastery, and strong support systems to enhance their motivation and job satisfaction.

Emily: "This experience has shown me how important it is to have control over my work, opportunities to grow, and a supportive team. I encourage everyone to find or create environments that foster these elements—it can make all the difference in staying motivated and satisfied in your career."

By applying SDT principles and giving Emily more control over her projects, providing targeted feedback to enhance her skills, and fostering a supportive team environment, her supervisor reignited Emily's intrinsic motivation, leading to improved performance and job satisfaction. This scenario highlights the importance of autonomy, mastery, and support in enhancing engagement and performance in the workplace.

Know Your Process

Coaching to performance is about more than just setting high standards and expecting results—it's about creating a structured, repeatable process that drives consistent success. By coaching your coachees to understand and master your processes, you empower them to achieve optimal performance and deliver outstanding results.

A well-defined process provides a roadmap for your coachees, outlining the steps they need to take to achieve their goals. It ensures that everyone is aligned, working efficiently, and focused on the right priorities. Your process is also a great starting point for building out the metrics that will measure performance improvement. You can track the leading indicators as your team works through their process and the lagging indicators as outcomes are achieved, giving you a comprehensive view of progress and areas for further enhancement. By continuously analyzing these metrics, you can identify patterns, adjust strategies, and ensure that your team remains on a path of continuous growth and success. As you coach your coachees to embrace and execute these processes, you help them build a foundation of discipline and consistency that supports their growth and success.

Teach your coachees the importance of process adherence by demonstrating how following established procedures leads to better outcomes. Use real-world examples and case studies to illustrate how a well-executed process can streamline workflows, reduce errors, and improve overall performance. *Encourage them to see the process as a tool for achieving their goals, rather than a rigid set of rules.*

In addition to teaching the existing processes, involve your coachees in continuous improvement initiatives. Encourage them to identify areas where the process can be refined or enhanced, and empower them to contribute their ideas. This collaborative approach not only improves the process itself but also fosters a sense of ownership and engagement among your coachees.

By coaching your coachees to know and execute the process, you also instill a mindset of accountability and responsibility. They learn to track their progress, measure their performance, and make data-driven decisions. This analytical approach helps them understand the impact of their actions and identify opportunities for further improvement.

Moreover, mastering the process equips your coachees with the confidence and competence to handle complex situations and unexpected challenges. They become adept at navigating obstacles, adapting to changing circumstances, and maintaining focus on their objectives. This resilience and adaptability are key to sustained high performance.

Ultimately, coaching to performance through a deep understanding of your processes ensures that your coachees are not just meeting expectations but exceeding them. It creates a culture of excellence where everyone is committed to continuous growth and improvement. By knowing your process and executing it flawlessly, your coachees can consistently deliver exceptional results and drive the success of your organization.

Call To Action

1. Identify a current obstacle faced by a coachee and brainstorm strategies to overcome it.

Your Notes:

_____

_____

_____

_____

_____

_____

_____

2. Encourage your coachee to set a personal motivation goal and track their progress.

Your Notes:

_____

_____

_____

_____

_____

_____

_____

3. Implement a resilience training session with your team to build their coping skills.

Your Notes:

_____

_____

_____

_____

_____

_____

4. Foster intrinsic motivation by enhancing autonomy, mastery, and purpose in your coachee's work.

Your Notes:

_____

_____

_____

_____

_____

_____

Attributions

The Five Whys Technique
- **Origin:** Developed by Sakichi Toyoda, used within Toyota Motor Corporation during the evolution of their manufacturing methodologies.
- **Usage:** To identify the root cause of a problem by repeatedly asking "Why?" until the underlying issue is uncovered.
- **Description:** This iterative interrogative technique helps drill down into the details of a problem by asking "Why?" at least

five times or until the root cause is identified. It's often used in conjunction with other analysis tools in quality management and problem-solving processes.

Fishbone Diagram (Ishikawa Diagram)
- **Origin:** Created by Kaoru Ishikawa in the 1960s.
- **Usage:** To visually display the potential causes of a specific problem, categorizing them into branches to identify the root cause.
- **Description:** The Fishbone Diagram, also known as the Ishikawa Diagram or Cause-and-Effect Diagram, organizes potential causes of problems into categories such as People, Methods, Machines, Materials, Measurements, and Environment. This visual tool helps teams brainstorm and systematically identify contributing factors.

Pareto Analysis
- **Origin:** Based on the Pareto Principle by Vilfredo Pareto, popularized by Joseph Juran in the context of quality management.
- **Usage:** To identify the most significant factors contributing to a problem by focusing on the "vital few" causes that account for the majority of the issues.
- **Description:** Pareto Analysis uses the 80/20 rule, suggesting that 80% of problems are often due to 20% of causes. It helps prioritize issues by identifying the most significant factors that need attention, typically visualized through Pareto charts.

Fault Tree Analysis (FTA)
- **Origin:** Developed by Bell Telephone Laboratories in the 1960s for the U.S. Air Force.
- **Usage:** To analyze the probability of system failures by identifying and examining the root causes in a logical tree format.

- **Description:** FTA is a top-down approach that starts with a potential undesirable event and branches out into all possible root causes using logic gates (AND, OR) to systematically identify failure paths and probabilities, enhancing reliability and safety analysis.

Root Cause Analysis (RCA)
- **Origin:** Evolved through the fields of quality control and accident investigation.
- **Usage:** A broad methodology to identify the root causes of problems or incidents, including tools like the Five Whys, Fishbone Diagram, and others.
- **Description:** RCA is a collective term for various methods and techniques used to discover the root causes of issues. It's widely used across industries to analyze accidents, failures, and non-conformance events, aiming to implement corrective actions to prevent recurrence.

Conclusion: Turning Challenges into Opportunities

Challenges and setbacks are a natural part of any journey, but how we address them defines our success. By building resilience and fostering intrinsic motivation, we can help our coachees navigate these obstacles and emerge stronger. As coaches, our role is to provide the tools, support, and encouragement needed to turn challenges into opportunities for growth and development.

Remember, overcoming obstacles is not just about finding solutions but about developing the mindset and skills to handle future challenges with confidence and grace. By applying the strategies discussed in this chapter, you can empower your coachees to face setbacks head-on and maintain their motivation, ultimately leading to sustained growth and success.

Thank you for joining me on this journey through *Performance Whisperer*. I hope the insights and techniques shared in this book have equipped you with the tools to unlock the full potential of those you lead. Now, it's time to put these strategies into practice and create a lasting impact on the lives and careers of your coachees.

Let's get started on creating a world where everyone reaches their highest potential through the power of coaching.

By incorporating resilience training and intrinsic motivation techniques, you can help your coachees overcome obstacles and stay motivated, leading to a culture of continuous improvement and excellence. Embrace challenges as opportunities, and guide your coachees towards sustained growth and success.

Part 4

Evolving Your Coaching Process as You Learn

CHAPTER 10

Leveraging Newly Acquired Skills to Evolve Your Coaching

I believe that to be an effective coach, one must always strive for continuous improvement. This chapter is dedicated to the skills and knowledge I've acquired throughout my journey. My personal development has been fueled by a commitment to lifelong learning, which includes a steady diet of reading and listening to insightful books and podcasts—I have many recommendations to share. In addition to self-study, I pursue regular certifications that require me to apply and demonstrate new knowledge and skills. Mentorship has also played a crucial role in my growth, providing a space where my thinking is challenged, my perspectives are broadened, and I receive invaluable feedback. All of these elements—self-study, certifications, and mentorship—are integral to my philosophy of continuous improvement and are reflected in my approach to coaching.

In this chapter, we will explore how to leverage the new skills I've built through certifications in Design Thinking, Change Management, and Executive Communication. These skills have become essential for fostering a culture of continuous improvement, effectively managing change, and ensuring clear and impactful communication within my coaching practice. As I take on new skills, my goal is to always apply them to my core competencies, including coaching. I challenge you to think of the skills you have built and how you can apply them to how you coach.

Design Thinking in Coaching

Design Thinking is a human-centered approach to problem-solving that emphasizes understanding the user, challenging assumptions, and redefining problems to identify alternative strategies and solutions.

Empathize: Understand Your Coachee's Needs

- Conduct one-on-one interviews to gather insights into your coachee's experiences, challenges, and aspirations.
- Use empathy maps to visualize their emotions, thoughts, and behaviors.

Example: Anna, a team lead, struggles with time management. By conducting empathy interviews, her coach discovers that Anna feels overwhelmed by her responsibilities and lacks effective prioritization skills. Using these insights, the coach develops a personalized strategy that addresses Anna's specific pain points.

Define: Clarify the Problem

- Synthesize the information gathered during the empathy phase to define the core problems.
- Create problem statements that are clear and focused.

Example: Anna's coach defines the problem statement: "Anna needs a way to manage her time effectively because she feels overwhelmed by her tasks, leading to decreased productivity and increased stress."

Ideate: Generate Ideas and Solutions

- Facilitate brainstorming sessions to explore a wide range of ideas and solutions.
- Encourage creativity and think outside the box.

Example: During a brainstorming session, Anna and her coach generate ideas such as implementing a time-blocking system, using task management software, and delegating non-essential tasks to her team.

Prototype: Develop Tangible Solutions

- Create small-scale prototypes of the potential solutions to test their viability.
- Encourage coachees to experiment with different approaches.

Example: Anna's coach helps her prototype a time-blocking system by scheduling her week in advance and setting specific times for different tasks. They also set up a trial period to test task management software.

Test: Evaluate and Iterate

- Test the prototypes with the coachee and gather feedback.
- Iterate based on the feedback to refine the solutions.

Example: Anna tests the time-blocking system and task management software for two weeks. She provides feedback to her coach, who then makes adjustments to better suit Anna's workflow. This iterative process continues until they find an optimal solution.

Call to Action:

1. Conduct an empathy interview with a coachee to understand their challenges and needs.
2. Define a clear problem statement based on the insights gathered.
3. Brainstorm potential solutions and create prototypes to test with your coachee.

Change Management in Coaching

Change Management involves preparing, supporting, and helping individuals, teams, and organizations in making organizational change. It's essential for coaches to understand how to manage change effectively to help their coachees adapt and thrive in new environments.

Prepare for Change

- Conduct a readiness assessment to determine the coachee's preparedness for change.
- Develop a clear vision and strategy for the change initiative.

Example: Mike, a sales manager, is implementing a new CRM system. His coach conducts a readiness assessment to gauge his team's readiness and develops a strategy to address potential resistance.

Support the Change

- Communicate the change effectively to ensure everyone understands the reasons, benefits, and impacts.
- Provide training and resources to help coachees develop the necessary skills and knowledge.

Example: Mike's coach helps him create a communication plan that includes regular updates and training sessions. They also develop a resource guide to assist the team in using the new CRM system.

Reinforce the Change

- Monitor the progress of the change initiative and gather feedback.
- Recognize and celebrate successes to reinforce positive behavior.

Example: Mike's coach sets up regular check-ins to monitor the team's progress and gathers feedback to identify areas for improvement. They also celebrate milestones to keep the team motivated.

Call to Action:

1. Conduct a readiness assessment for an upcoming change initiative with your coachee.
2. Develop a communication plan and resource guide to support the change.
3. Set up regular check-ins to monitor progress and gather feedback.

Executive Communication in Coaching

Executive Communication involves conveying messages in a clear, concise, and compelling manner. Effective communication skills are crucial for coaches to articulate their vision, provide feedback, and inspire their coachees.

Craft Clear Messages: Be Concise and Direct

- Focus on clarity and brevity when communicating with coachees.
- Avoid jargon and complex language.

Example: Samantha, a marketing director, needs to communicate a new strategy to her team. Her coach helps her craft a clear and concise message that outlines the key points and expected outcomes.

Engage the Audience: Use Storytelling

- Incorporate storytelling techniques to make messages more relatable and engaging.
- Use real-life examples and anecdotes.

Example: Samantha uses storytelling to explain the new strategy, sharing a success story from a previous campaign to illustrate the potential impact of the new approach.

Active Listening: Foster Two-Way Communication

- Practice active listening to understand the coachee's perspective and respond thoughtfully.
- Encourage open dialogue and feedback.

Example: Samantha's coach practices active listening during their sessions, ensuring she feels heard and valued. This fosters a collaborative environment where ideas can be freely exchanged.

Call to Action:

1. Craft a clear and concise message for an upcoming coaching session.
2. Use storytelling to make your message more engaging and relatable.
3. Practice active listening to foster open communication with your coachee.

Leveraging the skills of Design Thinking, Change Management, and Executive Communication can significantly enhance your coaching practice. These skills enable you to create innovative solutions, manage change effectively, and communicate with impact. By integrating these methodologies into your coaching, you can help your coachees navigate challenges, embrace change, and achieve their highest potential.

Thank you for joining me on this journey. Let's get started on creating a world where everyone reaches their highest potential through the power of coaching.

Call to Action:

1. Reflect on how you can integrate Design Thinking, Change Management, and Executive Communication into your coaching practice.
2. Identify a specific area in your coaching where you can apply these skills.

3. Develop a plan to implement these methodologies and observe the impact on your coachee's performance and development.

BONUS CONTENT

The Pyramid Principle: Structuring Your Thoughts for Clear Communication

Barbara Minto's Pyramid Principle is a framework for structuring your thoughts and ideas in a clear, logical manner. This method helps improve communication, making it easier for your audience to understand and retain information. The Pyramid Principle is especially useful for crafting compelling arguments, writing reports, and delivering presentations.

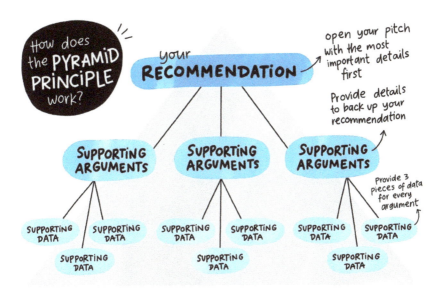

Importance of the Pyramid Principle

1. **Clarity:** Organizes ideas logically, making them easier to understand.
2. **Efficiency:** Saves time by presenting information in a structured way.
3. **Persuasion:** Builds compelling arguments that are easy to follow.

4. **Retention:** Helps your audience remember key points.

5. **Focus:** Ensures you stay on topic and cover all relevant aspects.

The Structure of the Pyramid Principle

1. **The Top of the Pyramid (Main Idea):**
   - **Purpose:** State the main idea or recommendation upfront.
   - **Example:** "We should implement a new customer relationship management (CRM) system to improve sales efficiency and customer satisfaction."

2. **The Middle Layer (Supporting Arguments):**
   - **Purpose:** Provide 3–5 key arguments or reasons that support the main idea.
   - **Example:**
     - **Argument 1:** A new CRM system will streamline sales processes.
     - **Argument 2:** It will enhance customer data management.
     - **Argument 3:** It will provide better analytics and reporting capabilities.

3. **The Base Layer (Supporting Details):**
   - **Purpose:** Offer detailed evidence and examples to back up each supporting argument.
   - **Example:**
     - **Argument 1:** Streamline Sales Processes
       - Details: Automated work Your Coaching Workbook
       - flows, centralized data access, improved lead tracking.
     - **Argument 2:** Enhance Customer Data Management
       - Details: Unified customer profiles, improved data accuracy, easier data updates.
     - **Argument 3:** Better Analytics and Reporting
       - Details: Advanced reporting tools, real-time analytics, customizable dashboards.

Steps to Apply the Pyramid Principle

1. **Define the Main Idea:** Clearly articulate the central message or recommendation you want to convey.
   - **Example:** "Implementing a new CRM system is essential for our sales growth."
2. **Identify Supporting Arguments:** Determine the key reasons or benefits that support your main idea.
   - **Example:**
     - "A new CRM system will streamline our sales processes."
     - "It will enhance our customer data management."
     - "It will provide better analytics and reporting capabilities."
3. **Develop Supporting Details:** Gather detailed evidence, examples, and data to substantiate each supporting argument.
   - **Example:**
     - **Streamline Sales Processes:** Automated workflows, centralized data access, improved lead tracking.
     - **Enhance Customer Data Management:** Unified customer profiles, improved data accuracy, easier data updates.
     - **Better Analytics and Reporting:** Advanced reporting tools, real-time analytics, customizable dashboards.
4. **Organize in a Hierarchical Structure:** Arrange your main idea, supporting arguments, and supporting details in a hierarchical pyramid format.
   - **Example:**
     - **Top:** Implementing a new CRM system is essential for our sales growth.
     - **Middle:** Streamline sales processes, enhance customer data management, better analytics and reporting.
     - **Base:** Detailed evidence for each supporting argument.

5. **Refine and Simplify:** Review your pyramid structure to ensure clarity, logical flow, and conciseness. Simplify complex information and remove any redundant details.
   - ◦ **Example:**
     - ▪ "Implementing a new CRM system will streamline our sales processes, enhance customer data management, and provide better analytics and reporting."

Common Techniques for Applying the Pyramid Principle

1. **MECE Principle (Mutually Exclusive, Collectively Exhaustive):**
   - ◦ **Origin:** Developed by Barbara Minto.
   - ◦ **Usage:** Ensure that each supporting argument is distinct (mutually exclusive) and that all possible arguments are covered (collectively exhaustive).
   - ◦ **Example:**
     - ▪ Argument 1: CRM streamlines processes.
     - ▪ Argument 2: CRM enhances data management.
     - ▪ Argument 3: CRM improves analytics.
     - ▪ No overlap between arguments, and all major benefits are covered.

2. **Chunking:**
   - ◦ **Origin:** Cognitive psychology concept.
   - ◦ **Usage:** Break down complex information into manageable chunks to improve understanding and retention.
   - ◦ **Example:**
     - ▪ Main Idea: New CRM system.
     - ▪ Chunk 1: Sales process improvements.
     - ▪ Chunk 2: Data management enhancements.
     - ▪ Chunk 3: Advanced analytics.

3. **SCQA Framework (Situation, Complication, Question, Answer):**
   - ◦ **Origin:** Developed by Barbara Minto.

- Usage: Structure the introduction of your pyramid by outlining the context (Situation), the problem (Complication), the key question, and the solution (Answer).

Example:

- Situation: Our current sales process is inefficient.
- Complication: This inefficiency is leading to lost sales opportunities.
- Question: How can we improve our sales process?
- Answer: Implement a new CRM system.

4. **Top-Down Communication:**
   - **Origin:** Management communication practice.
   - **Usage:** Start with the main idea or conclusion first, followed by supporting arguments and details.
   - **Example:**
     - Start with: "We need a new CRM system."
     - Then: "Here's why: it streamlines processes, enhances data management, and improves analytics."

5. **Bullet Pointing:**
   - **Origin:** Common writing technique.
   - **Usage:** Use bullet points to list supporting arguments and details clearly and concisely.
   - **Example:**
     - Implementing a new CRM system will:
       - Streamline our sales processes.
       - Enhance customer data management.
       - Provide better analytics and reporting.

Attributions

Design Thinking
- **Origin:** Developed by David Kelley and Tim Brown at IDEO in the late 1990s.

- **Usage:** Widely used in product development, problem-solving, and innovation.
- **Description:** Design Thinking is a human-centered approach to problem-solving that involves understanding the user, challenging assumptions, and redefining problems. It includes five phases: Empathize, Define, Ideate, Prototype, and Test.

Change Management
- **Origin:** Popularized by John Kotter in the 1990s with his 8-Step Change Model.
- **Usage:** Used to manage organizational change effectively, ensuring smooth transitions and employee buy-in.
- **Description:** Change Management involves preparing, supporting, and helping individuals, teams, and organizations in making organizational change. Key components include readiness assessment, communication planning, training, and reinforcement.

Executive Communication
- **Origin:** Developed through various leadership and management theories, with significant contributions from experts like Peter Drucker and John C. Maxwell.
- **Usage:** Essential for conveying messages clearly and persuasively at the executive level.
- **Description:** Executive Communication involves conveying messages in a clear, concise, and compelling manner. It includes skills such as crafting clear messages, storytelling, and active listening to ensure effective two-way communication.

Pyramid Principle
- **Origin:** Developed by Barbara Minto at McKinsey & Company in the 1960s.

- **Usage:** To structure ideas and arguments in a clear, hierarchical manner for effective communication.
- **Description:** The Pyramid Principle organizes information into a logical structure starting with the main idea, followed by supporting points grouped into categories. This top-down approach helps present complex information clearly and concisely, facilitating better understanding and decision-making.

MECE Principle (Mutually Exclusive, Collectively Exhaustive)
- **Origin:** Developed at McKinsey & Company, often associated with Barbara Minto.
- **Usage:** Ensures that categories or elements of an argument are non-overlapping and cover all possibilities.
- **Description:** The MECE Principle is used to break down information into distinct, non-overlapping categories that collectively cover all potential areas. It helps in structuring data analysis, problem-solving, and strategic planning by ensuring completeness and clarity.

Chunking
- **Origin:** Concept from cognitive psychology, studied by George A. Miller in the 1950s.
- **Usage:** To break down complex information into smaller, manageable units to improve understanding and retention.
- **Description:** Chunking involves organizing information into bite-sized pieces or "chunks" to make it easier to process and remember. This technique is widely used in learning, memory training, and information presentation to enhance cognitive efficiency.

SCQA Framework (Situation, Complication, Question, Answer)
- **Origin:** Part of the Pyramid Principle by Barbara Minto.
- **Usage:** To structure the introduction of a pyramid by outlining the context, problem, key question, and solution.

- **Description:** The SCQA Framework helps set the stage for presenting ideas by first describing the Situation, then the Complication or problem, followed by the central Question that needs addressing, and finally the Answer or solution. This structured approach engages the audience and sets a clear path for the argument.

Top-Down Communication
- **Origin:** Management communication practice popularized in business strategy.
- **Usage:** Present the main idea or conclusion first, followed by supporting arguments and details.
- **Description:** Top-Down Communication starts with the most important message or conclusion and then provides supporting details. This method ensures that key points are communicated clearly and quickly, making it easier for audiences to grasp the main idea upfront.

Bullet Pointing
- **Origin:** Common writing technique used in business and academic writing.
- **Usage:** To list supporting arguments and details clearly and concisely.
- **Description:** Bullet Pointing involves using bullet points to present information in a clear, organized manner. It enhances readability and helps highlight key points, making complex information more accessible and easier to understand.

Conclusion

As we reach the end of *Performance Whisperer*, I hope you feel as inspired and empowered as I do about the transformative power of coaching. Throughout this book, we've delved deep into the fundamental principles of effective coaching, explored practical techniques, and shared stories that illustrate the profound impact coaching can have on individuals and organizations.

Coaching is an ongoing journey of growth, both for the coach and the coachee. It's about continuously learning, adapting, and striving to bring out the best in ourselves and others. By focusing on empathy, skill development, and performance improvement, we can create environments where individuals feel valued, motivated, and equipped to achieve their goals.

Remember, coaching is not just about providing answers; it's about asking the right questions, listening deeply, and fostering a sense of trust and collaboration. It's about helping others see their potential, guiding them through challenges, and celebrating their successes.

In this book, we've also explored how to leverage Design Thinking, Change Management, and Executive Communication to enhance your coaching practice. These methodologies have provided us with innovative ways to approach problem-solving, manage change effectively, and communicate with impact. Integrating these skills into your coaching toolkit will enable you to navigate challenges more effectively and inspire your coachees to reach their highest potential.

As you move forward in your coaching journey, keep these key takeaways in mind:

- **Coaching Like a Human:** Always approach coaching with empathy and understanding. Connect with the human behind the performance and build relationships based on trust and mutual respect.

- **Coaching Skill:** Invest in your own continuous development as a coach. Stay curious, keep learning, and seek out new techniques and strategies to enhance your coaching practice.
- **Coaching Performance:** Set clear goals, provide constructive feedback, and celebrate progress. Help those you coach to stay focused, motivated, and committed to their growth.

At the beginning of this book I stated that my enablement philosophy is rooted in three core principles: know your customers, know your products, and know your process. By deeply understanding these elements, you can tailor your coaching approach to meet the unique needs of each coachee and drive meaningful results for your business.

First, coaching to empathy is crucial for truly knowing your customers. Building trust and deep connections with coachees begins with active listening and emotional intelligence. Practicing active listening techniques like maintaining eye contact and summarizing what the coachee says helps improve understanding and rapport. Developing emotional intelligence enhances your ability to manage emotions and respond empathetically, ensuring that your coaching is supportive and impactful. This approach allows you to see the world through your coachee's eyes, fostering stronger relationships and more effective coaching outcomes.

Second, coaching to skill is essential for mastering knowledge about your products or what you sell. Conducting assessments like SWOT analysis and 360-degree feedback helps identify strengths and weaknesses. Creating personalized development plans with SMART goals and implementing skill-building activities such as workshops and training sessions ensures continuous growth. Providing specific, actionable feedback using frameworks like the SBI model enables coachees to understand areas for improvement and excel in their roles. By honing their product knowledge and skills, you empower your coachees to become experts in their field, driving better business results.

Lastly, coaching to performance by knowing and executing a tight process is key to achieving consistent success. Establishing clear, achievable SMART goals aligned with organizational objectives provides direction and focus. Breaking down these goals into actionable steps with defined deadlines ensures a structured approach to achieving them. Implementing continuous improvement initiatives like Kaizen and the PDCA cycle fosters a culture of ongoing development and excellence. Identifying potential obstacles and developing strategies to overcome them, coupled with using intrinsic motivation techniques, helps maintain engagement and drive sustained performance. By focusing on a well-defined process, you ensure that your coaching leads to measurable and impactful outcomes.

In closing, I want to express my deepest gratitude for allowing me to share my vision and experiences with you. I hope this book has provided you with valuable insights and practical tools that you can apply in your coaching practice. Together, we can create a world where coaching is not just a profession but a way of life—a way to inspire, empower, and elevate others to reach their fullest potential.

Performance Whisperer is more than just a book; it's a blueprint for becoming a catalyst for change and growth. By embracing empathy, honing your coaching skills, and focusing on performance, you have the power to transform not only the individuals you coach but also your organization.

Now that you have the tools and insights to become an exceptional coach, it's time to put them into practice. Start by assessing your current coaching relationships and identifying areas for improvement. Implement the strategies discussed in this book, and observe the positive changes in your coachees' performance and development. Share your journey and experiences with others to create a ripple effect of transformative coaching.

As I reflect on my own journey, from my early days as an opera singer to my current role in enablement, I've seen firsthand the incredible impact that effective coaching can have. It's a journey that requires dedication, empathy, and a commitment to continuous improvement. But the rewards are immeasurable—both for you and for those you coach.

Thank you for embarking on this journey with me. Let's get started on creating a world where everyone reaches their highest potential through the power of coaching.

Your Coaching Workbook

The Empathy Framework

Purpose: Build trust and deepen connections with coachees by fostering empathy.

Steps:

1. **Active Listening:**
   - **Description:** Fully concentrate on what the coachee is saying without interrupting. Use body language and verbal cues to show engagement.
   - **Techniques:**
     - Maintain eye contact.
     - Nod to show understanding.
     - Summarize and paraphrase what the coachee says to confirm understanding.
   - **Outcome:** Improved understanding of the coachee's perspective and stronger rapport.

2. **Template:**
   - Session Date:
   - Coachee Name:
   - Key Points Summarized:
   - Observations on Coachee's Emotions and Reactions:

3. **Emotional Intelligence:**
   - **Description:** Be aware of your own emotions and recognize the emotions of others. Use this awareness to manage your interactions empathetically.
   - **Techniques:**
     - Self-reflection exercises.
     - Practicing mindfulness.
     - Observing and interpreting body language.
   - **Outcome:** Enhanced ability to manage emotions and respond empathetically.

4. **Template:**
   - Emotion Identification (Self):
   - Emotion Identification (Coachee):
   - Strategies Used to Manage Emotions:
5. **Empathy Mapping:**
   - **Description:** Use empathy maps to visualize the coachee's feelings, thoughts, and experiences.
   - **Techniques:**
   - Create quadrants for what the coachee says, thinks, feels, and does.
     - Fill in the map based on your observations and conversations.
   - **Outcome:** Clearer insight into the coachee's needs and motivations.
6. **Template:**
   - Empathy Map for [Coachee Name]:
     - Says:
     - Thinks:
     - Feels:
     - Does:
7. **Trust-Building Activities:**
   - **Description:** Engage in activities that build trust, such as sharing personal experiences, being transparent, and showing reliability.
   - **Techniques:**
     - Share a personal story related to a coachee's experience.
     - Be transparent about your intentions and decisions.
     - Follow through on commitments.
   - **Outcome:** Stronger, more trusting relationships with coachees.
8. **Template:**
   - Trust-Building Activity Conducted:
   - Coachee's Response:
   - Follow-Up Actions:

9. **Feedback Loop:**
   - **Description:** Regularly seek feedback from coachees about your coaching style and make adjustments based on their input.
   - **Techniques:**
     - Use surveys or direct questions.
     - Discuss feedback openly and plan improvements.
   - **Outcome:** Continuous improvement in your empathy and coaching effectiveness.
10. **Template:**
    - Feedback Collected:
    - Adjustments Made:
    - Outcomes Observed:

The Skill Development Framework

Purpose: Identify strengths and weaknesses, tailor development plans, and provide constructive feedback.

Steps:
1. **Strengths and Weaknesses Assessment:**
   - **Description:** Conduct assessments such as SWOT analysis or 360-degree feedback.
   - Techniques:
     - Use surveys, interviews, and self-assessment tools.
     - Analyze the collected data to identify key strengths and weaknesses.
   - **Outcome:** Clear understanding of coachee's strengths and areas for improvement.
2. **Template:**
   - Assessment Method Used:
   - Strengths Identified:
   - Weaknesses Identified:

1. **Personalized Development Plan:**
   - ◦ **Description:** Create a customized development plan with SMART goals.
   - ◦ **Techniques:**
     - ▪ Set Specific, Measurable, Achievable, Relevant, and Time-bound goals.
     - ▪ Align goals with coachee's career aspirations and organizational objectives.
   - ◦ **Outcome:** Focused and actionable roadmap for professional growth.
2. **Template:**
   - ◦ SMART Goals Set:
   - ◦ Action Steps:
   - ◦ Timeline:
   - ◦ Progress Checkpoints:
3. **Skill-Building Activities:**
   - ◦ **Description:** Design and implement skill-building activities such as workshops, training sessions, and hands-on projects.
   - ◦ **Techniques:**
     - ▪ Identify necessary skills and design relevant activities.
     - ▪ Schedule regular training and practice sessions.
   - ◦ **Outcome:** Enhanced skills and competencies.
4. **Template:**
   - ◦ Skill to Develop:
   - ◦ Activity Designed:
   - ◦ Schedule:
   - ◦ Outcomes:
5. **Constructive Feedback:**
   - ◦ **Description:** Provide specific, actionable, and timely feedback using frameworks like the SBI model.
   - ◦ **Techniques:**
     - ▪ Use Situation-Behavior-Impact (SBI) model.
     - ▪ Ensure feedback is clear, constructive, and focused on improvement.

- **Outcome:** Improved performance and clear understanding of areas for growth.

6. **Template:**
   - Feedback Provided:
   - Situation:
   - Behavior:
   - Impact:
   - Action Plan:

7. **Regular Check-Ins:**
   - **Description:** Schedule regular check-ins to monitor progress and adjust development plans as needed.
   - **Techniques:**
     - Set regular meeting times.
     - Review progress and adjust plans based on coachee's needs.
   - **Outcome:** Continuous development and alignment with goals.

8. **Template:**
   - Check-In Date:
   - Progress Reviewed:
   - Adjustments Made:
   - Next Steps:

The Performance Improvement Framework

Purpose: Set goals, foster continuous improvement, and maintain motivation.

Steps:

1. **Goal Setting:**
   - **Description:** Set specific, measurable, achievable, relevant, and time-bound (SMART) goals aligned with broader organizational objectives.

- ◦ **Techniques:**
  - ▪ Collaborate with coachee to define SMART goals.
  - ▪ Ensure goals are aligned with the organization's strategic objectives.
- ◦ **Outcome:** Clear, actionable, and aligned goals.

2. **Template:**
   - ◦ SMART Goals:
   - ◦ Alignment with Organizational Objectives:
   - ◦ Progress Metrics:

3. **Action Planning:**
   - ◦ **Description:** Break down goals into actionable steps with clear deadlines and responsibilities.
   - ◦ **Techniques:**
     - ▪ Develop a step-by-step plan to achieve each goal.
     - ▪ Assign responsibilities and set deadlines.
   - ◦ **Outcome:** Detailed roadmap to achieve goals.

4. **Template:**
   - ◦ Goal:
   - ◦ Action Steps:
   - ◦ Responsibilities:
   - ◦ Deadlines:

5. **Continuous Improvement Initiatives:**
   - ◦ **Description:** Implement continuous improvement initiatives such as Kaizen and the PDCA cycle.
   - ◦ **Techniques:**
     - ▪ Identify areas for improvement.
     - ▪ Plan and implement small, incremental changes.
     - ▪ Use the Plan-Do-Check-Act (PDCA) cycle for ongoing improvements.
   - ◦ **Outcome:** Ongoing improvement and enhanced performance.

6. **Template:**
   - Improvement Area:
   - Initiative Planned:
   - PDCA Cycle Steps:
     - Plan:
     - Do:
     - Check:
     - Act:

7. **Overcoming Obstacles:**
   - **Description:** Identify potential obstacles and develop strategies to overcome them.
   - Techniques:
     - Discuss potential challenges with coachee.
     - Brainstorm and implement strategies to overcome obstacles.
   - **Outcome:** Preparedness and resilience in facing challenges.

8. **Template:**
   - Obstacle Identified:
   - Strategy Developed:
   - Implementation Plan:
   - Outcome:

9. **Maintaining Motivation:**
   - **Description:** Use intrinsic motivation techniques such as fostering autonomy, mastery, and purpose to keep coachees motivated.
   - **Techniques:**
     - Provide opportunities for autonomy in tasks.
     - Encourage mastery through skill development.
     - Connect tasks to a larger purpose.
   - **Outcome:** Sustained motivation and engagement.

10. **Template:**
    - Motivation Techniques Used:
    - Coachee's Response:
    - Outcomes Observed:

Coaching Strategy Template

Title: Your Coaching Strategy

Introduction: Briefly describe the purpose of your coaching strategy and what you aim to achieve through it.

Part 1: Coaching Like a Human (Focusing on Empathy)

Chapter 1: The Heart of Coaching
- **Description:** Define empathy and its role in your coaching approach.
- **Examples:**
  - Example 1:
  - Example 2:
- **Progress & Outcomes:**
  - Progress 1:
  - Progress 2:
- **Call to Action:**
  - Identify a recent coaching session and reflect on how empathy was (or wasn't) demonstrated.
  - Write down two ways you can incorporate more empathy into your next coaching conversation.

Chapter 2: Building Trust and Rapport
- **Description:** Outline techniques for building trust and rapport with coachees.
- **Examples:**
  - Example 1:
  - Example 2:
- **Progress & Outcomes:**
  - Progress 1:
  - Progress 2:

- **Call to Action:**
  - Plan a trust-building activity with a coachee (e.g., share a personal story or acknowledge a shared challenge).
  - Ask your coachee for feedback on your relationship and take actionable steps based on their input.

Chapter 3: Active Listening
- **Description:** Highlight the importance of active listening in your coaching practice.
- **Examples:**
  - Example 1:
  - Example 2:
- **Progress & Outcomes:**
  - Progress 1:
  - Progress 2:
- **Call to Action:**
  - Practice active listening techniques (e.g., paraphrasing, asking open-ended questions) in your next coaching session.
  - Record a coaching conversation (with permission) and review it to assess your listening skills.

Part 2: Coaching Skill (Focusing on Professional Development)

Chapter 4: Identifying Strengths and Weaknesses
- **Description:** Describe your methods for identifying and leveraging individual strengths and addressing weaknesses.
- **Examples:**
  - Example 1:
  - Example 2:
- **Progress & Outcomes:**
  - Progress 1:
  - Progress 2:

- **Call to Action:**
  - Conduct a strengths and weaknesses assessment (e.g., SWOT analysis) with a coachee.
  - Schedule a follow-up meeting to discuss the results and create an action plan.

Chapter 5: Tailoring Development Plans
- **Description:** Explain how you will create personalized development plans for your coachees.
- **Examples:**
  - Example 1:
  - Example 2:
- **Progress & Outcomes:**
  - Progress 1:
  - Progress 2:
- **Call to Action:**
  - Draft a personalized development plan for one of your coachees using SMART goals.
  - Review the plan with your coachee and agree on next steps.

Chapter 6: Providing Constructive Feedback
- **Description:** Discuss your approach to giving feedback that motivates and guides improvement.
- **Examples:**
  - Example 1:
  - Example 2:
- **Progress & Outcomes:**
  - Progress 1:
  - Progress 2:
- **Call to Action:**
  - Use the SBI (Situation-Behavior-Impact) model to prepare for your next feedback session.
  - Deliver feedback to a coachee and ask for their thoughts on its effectiveness.

Part 3: Coaching Performance (Goal Setting and Continuous Improvement)

Chapter 7: Setting SMART Goals
- **Description:** Introduce the SMART criteria for setting goals with your coachees.
- **Examples:**
  - Example 1:
  - Example 2:
- **Progress & Outcomes:**
  - Progress 1:
  - Progress 2:
- **Call to Action:**
  - Work with a coachee to set three SMART goals related to their professional development.
  - Schedule regular check-ins to monitor progress towards these goals.

Chapter 8: Creating a Culture of Continuous Improvement
- **Description:** Discuss your strategies for fostering a culture of continuous improvement.
- **Examples:**
  - Example 1:
  - Example 2:
- **Progress & Outcomes:**
  - Progress 1:
  - Progress 2:
- **Call to Action:**
  - Implement a continuous improvement initiative (e.g., a weekly learning session) with your team.
  - Collect feedback on the initiative's impact and make necessary adjustments.

Chapter 9: Overcoming Obstacles and Staying Motivated

- **Description:** Outline common challenges and your strategies for overcoming them and maintaining motivation.
- **Examples:**
  - Example 1:
  - Example 2:
- **Progress & Outcomes:**
  - Progress 1:
  - Progress 2:
- **Call to Action:**
  - Identify a current obstacle faced by a coachee and brainstorm strategies to overcome it.
  - Encourage your coachee to set a personal motivation goal and track their progress.

Coaching Profile Outline for Coachee

Coachee Name:

Introduction:

- Brief background of the coachee.
- Goals of the coaching relationship.

Part 1: Empathy and Trust Building

Empathy Mapping:

- Visual representation of the coachee's feelings, thoughts, and experiences.

Trust-Building Activities:

- Document specific activities undertaken to build trust.

Part 2: Skill Development

Strengths and Weaknesses Assessment:

- Summary of the assessment results.

Personalized Development Plan:
- Detailed plan with SMART goals and action steps.

Part 3: Performance Improvement
Goal Setting:
- List of SMART goals set with the coachee.

Continuous Improvement Initiatives:
- Documentation of initiatives and their impact.

Overcoming Obstacles:
- Strategies developed and implemented to overcome specific challenges.

Motivation Maintenance:
- Techniques used to sustain the coachee's motivation.

Conclusion:
- Summary of progress and outcomes achieved.
- Next steps and future goals.

This template serves as a structured guide to help you organize and document your coaching relationships effectively. It ensures you cover all essential aspects of coaching, from building empathy and trust to developing skills and improving performance.

Coaching Profile Outline

Section	Details
Coachee Information	
Name	
Role/Position	
Department/Team	
Date of Initial Coaching Session	
Introduction	
Background	
Coaching Goals	
Part 1: Empathy and Trust Building	
Empathy Mapping	
Feelings	
Thoughts	
Experiences	
Trust-Building Activities	
Activity 1	
Activity 2	
Feedback from Coachee	
Adjustments Made	
Part 2: Skill Development	
Strengths and Weaknesses Assessment	
Strengths	
Weaknesses	
Assessment Method Used	
Personalized Development Plan	
Career Goals	
Current Skills and Competencies	
Development Objectives	
Action Plan	
Timeline	
Monitoring and Evaluation	

Section	Details
Part 3: Performance Improvement	
Goal Setting	
SMART Goal 1	
SMART Goal 2	
SMART Goal 3	
Continuous Improvement Initiatives	
Initiative 1	
Initiative 2	
Feedback and Adjustments	
Overcoming Obstacles	
Identified Obstacles	
Strategies Developed	
Implementation Plan	
Maintaining Motivation	
Motivation Techniques Used	
Progress and Outcomes	
Conclusion	
Summary of Progress	
Outcomes Achieved	
Next Steps	

Here is a lightweight template designed to help manage weekly coaching conversations effectively. This template focuses on essential elements to track progress, address challenges, set goals, and plan action steps.

Weekly Coaching Conversation Template

Section	Details
Coachee Information	
Name	
Role/Position	
Department/Team	
Date of Session	
Review of Last Week	
Goals Set Last Week	
Progress on Goals	
Achievements	
Challenges Faced	
Current Week Focus	
New Goals for the Week	
Priority Areas	
Key Discussion Points	
Topics Discussed	
Insights and Feedback	
Action Plan	
Actions to be Taken	
Responsible Party	
Deadline/Timeline	
Support Needed	
Resources/Support Required	
Next Steps	
Summary of Agreed Actions	
Next Meeting Date	

Instructions for Use

1. **Coachee Information:** Fill in the coachee's basic information at the start of each session.
2. **Review of Last Week:** Discuss and document the progress made on the goals set in the previous session. Note any achievements and challenges faced.
3. **Current Week Focus:** Set new goals for the current week, highlighting the priority areas.
4. **Key Discussion Points:** Summarize the main topics discussed during the session, including any insights or feedback given.
5. **Action Plan:** Clearly outline the actions to be taken, who is responsible for each action, and the deadlines or timelines for completion.
6. **Support Needed:** Identify any resources or support the coachee needs to achieve their goals.
7. **Next Steps:** Summarize the agreed-upon actions and set the date for the next meeting.

References

Empathy:
1. Rogers, C. R., & Farson, R. E. (1957). *Active Listening.* Industrial Relations Center of the University of Chicago.
2. Goleman, D. (1995). *Emotional Intelligence: Why It Can Matter More Than IQ.* Bantam Books.

Building Trust and Rapport:
1. Covey, S. M. R., & Merrill, R. R. (2006). *The Speed of Trust: The One Thing That Changes Everything.* Free Press.
2. Tschannen-Moran, M. (2004). *Trust Matters: Leadership for Successful Schools.* Jossey-Bass.

Active Listening:
1. Rogers, C. R., & Farson, R. E. (1957). *Active Listening.* Industrial Relations Center of the University of Chicago.
2. Brownell, J. (2012). *Listening: Attitudes, Principles, and Skills* (5th ed.). Pearson.

Identifying Strengths and Weaknesses:
1. Rath, T. (2007). *StrengthsFinder 2.0.* Gallup Press.
2. Buckingham, M., & Clifton, D. O. (2001). *Now, Discover Your Strengths.* Free Press.

Tailoring Development Plans:
1. Doran, G. T. (1981). "There's a S.M.A.R.T. Way to Write Management's Goals and Objectives". *Management Review.*
2. Noe, R. A. (2013). *Employee Training and Development* (6th ed.). McGraw-Hill Education.

Constructive Feedback:

1. Center for Creative Leadership. (2003). *Feedback That Works: How to Build and Deliver Your Message.* CCL Press.
2. Stone, D., & Heen, S. (2014). *Thanks for the Feedback: The Science and Art of Receiving Feedback Well.* Viking.

Setting SMART Goals:

1. Doran, G. T. (1981). "There's a S.M.A.R.T. Way to Write Management's Goals and Objectives". *Management Review.*
2. Blanchard, K. H., & Johnson, S. (1981). *The One Minute Manager.* William Morrow.

Creating a Culture of Continuous Improvement:

1. Imai, M. (1986). *Kaizen: The Key to Japan's Competitive Success.* McGraw-Hill.
2. Deming, W. E. (1986). *Out of the Crisis.* MIT Press.

Overcoming Obstacles and Staying Motivated:

1. Seligman, M. E. P. (1990). *Learned Optimism: How to Change Your Mind and Your Life.* Knopf.
2. Deci, E. L., & Ryan, R. M. (1985). *Intrinsic Motivation and Self-Determination in Human Behavior.* Plenum.

Design Thinking, Change Management, and Executive Communication:

1. Brown, T. (2009). *Change by Design: How Design Thinking Creates New Alternatives for Business and Society.* Harper Business.
2. Kotter, J. P. (1996). *Leading Change.* Harvard Business Review Press.
3. Duarte, N. (2010). *Resonate: Present Visual Stories that Transform Audiences.* Wiley.

Pyramid Principle:

1. Minto, B. (1987). *The Pyramid Principle: Logic in Writing and Thinking*. Minto International.

MECE Principle (Mutually Exclusive Collectively Exhaustive):

1. Developed at McKinsey & Company, often associated with Barbara Minto.

Chunking:

1. Concept from cognitive psychology, studied by George A. Miller in the 1950s.

SCQA Framework (Situation Complication Question Answer):

1. Part of the Pyramid Principle by Barbara Minto.

Top-Down Communication:

1. Management communication practice popularized in business strategy.

Bullet Pointing:

1. Common writing technique used in business and academic writing.

Root Cause Analysis:

1. The Five Whys Technique: Developed by Sakichi Toyoda, used within Toyota Motor Corporation.
2. Fishbone Diagram (Ishikawa Diagram): Created by Kaoru Ishikawa in the 1960s.
3. Pareto Analysis: Based on the Pareto Principle by Vilfredo Pareto, popularized by Joseph Juran.
4. Fault Tree Analysis (FTA): Developed by Bell Telephone Laboratories in the 1960s.
5. Root Cause Analysis (RCA): Evolved through the fields of quality control and accident investigation.

Techniques for Building Resilience:

1. Cognitive Behavioral Therapy (CBT) techniques.

SMART Goals:

1. Origin: First mentioned by George T. Doran in 1981.

OKRs (Objectives and Key Results):

1. Origin: Developed by Andy Grove at Intel in the 1970s.

Acknowledgements

As I conclude *Performance Whisperer*, I am filled with gratitude for the many individuals who have supported and inspired me throughout this journey.

First and foremost, I want to dedicate this book to Priscilla Winley, my former manager at Toshiba Corporation. Though you are no longer with us, your unwavering belief in my potential, your challenging yet supportive coaching, and your commitment to holding me to higher standards not only unlocked my potential but also gave me the freedom to forge my own path. Your influence has been instrumental in shaping my coaching philosophy and my approach to leadership. Your legacy continues to inspire me every day.

To my mentor, Steve Richard, thank you for teaching me that coaching was one of my superpowers. Your guidance has been invaluable in helping me realize my passion and potential in this field. Thank you for giving me a voice and so many opportunities to share my coaching vision.

I am deeply grateful to Anna Vuong, my manager, who not only helped cultivate my coaching skills but also provided me with a role where coaching became my full focus. Your support and encouragement have been pivotal in my professional growth.

To my sales and enablement family of practitioners—Celia Shore, Nate Slayton, Adam Behrens, Adam Hudson, Stephanie Middaugh, Elizabeth Noyes, Allison Butler, Shawn Fowler, Matt Haney, Brooke Smith, Dan Straus, Jon Ebner, and so many more—thank you for your camaraderie, insights, and shared experiences. Working alongside such dedicated professionals has enriched my journey and contributed immensely to this book.

To my partner, Tony, your love, patience, and unwavering support have been my rock. Thank you for always believing in me and encouraging me to pursue my passions. Our three dogs—Wick, Maya Rudolph, and Benny Hartz—who have been constant companions during late-night writing sessions, have brought joy and balance to my life.

To my friends and family, thank you for your encouragement and for being my sounding board. Your support has been invaluable, and your faith in me has kept me motivated throughout this process.

I would also like to extend my appreciation to the many authors, researchers, and thought leaders whose work has informed and inspired this book. Your contributions to the fields of coaching, leadership, and personal development have provided a solid foundation for the ideas and strategies presented here.

Finally, to my readers, thank you for embarking on this journey with me. I hope *Performance Whisperer* provides you with the tools, insights, and inspiration to unlock the full potential of those you lead. Your commitment to continuous improvement and your dedication to fostering growth and development in others is what truly makes a difference.

Here's to unlocking potential, driving performance, and creating a culture of continuous improvement together.

Milton Keynes UK
Ingram Content Group UK Ltd.
UKHW051645081024
449373UK00019B/309